Breads

BREADS

Editorial Director
DONALD D. WOLF

Design and Layout
MARGOT L. WOLF

Published by
LEXICON PUBLICATIONS, INC.
387 Park Avenue South, New York, NY 10016

Cover illustration:
French Bread, 10

Opposite title page:
Irish Soda Bread, 60

ISBN: 0-7172-4517-9

Contents

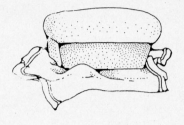

Bread and life, home, and hospitality are inextricably associated in the human imagination and experience. Old as history, breadmaking was one of the first culinary arts practiced—and at a time when home itself was little more than a few flat stones arranged round a fire. Now most of the peoples of the earth have breads characteristically their own. In our own country we have no single traditional bread. We have, instead, welcomed the traditions of all the peoples that have come here and made them our own. Made with or without leavening, bread appears in a hundred different, delightful guises—as soft loaves and crusty loaves, holiday breads and coffee cakes, waffles, griddlecakes, popovers, muffins and doughnuts, and in other forms too numerous to mention.

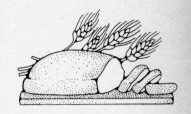

Yeast Breads

YEAST: grows in the presence of a given amount of moisture and sugar at a temperature of about 80°F, producing in the process tiny bubbles of carbon dioxide gas which leaven the bread dough. A dough must be leavened to rise and become light.

Compressed Yeast (*moist cake*)—Grayish tan though may be slightly browned at edges; breaks with a clean edge and crumbles easily between the fingers when fresh; must be kept in refrigerator and used within a week for best results; soften in lukewarm liquid (80°F to 85°F).

Active Dry Yeast—May be kept without refrigeration; to obtain best results use before date on package expires; one package when softened has the leavening power of one cake compressed yeast; soften in warm water (110°F to 115°F) only.

FLOUR—All-purpose flour is used for breadmaking in the home. The moisture content of flour varies with changes in humidity and also from one flour to another. To allow for this difference and to obtain the desired consistency of the dough, indefinite amounts of flour are given in recipes.

A small amount of flour (about 1 cup) is added to the fat-liquid mixture before the softened yeast is added to prevent the yeast from becoming coated with fat. Fat tends to retard the growth of yeast.

LIQUID—Water and milk are the liquids most commonly used in bread doughs. Fluid milk must be scalded before using in breadmaking. Evaporated milk does not need to be scalded because it has been preheated. The liquid must be hot enough to melt the shortening when added to shortening-sugar-salt mixture. For optimum yeast growth, this mixture, plus a small amount of flour, must be *lukewarm* (80°F) when softened yeast is added.

REFRIGERATOR DOUGHS are richer and sweeter than plain bread dough and can be successfully kept in the refrigerator (45° to 50°F) three to four days. Place dough in the refrigerator immediately after mixing kneading or after the first rising period (be sure it does not rise too much). Dough must be punched down occasionally if it rises during refrigeration. The dough is greased and well covered to keep the surface of the dough moist and elastic. When ready to bake, remove dough from refrigerator, shape, allow to rise until light and doubled before baking.

KNEAD DOUGH by folding opposite side over toward you. Using heels of hands, gently push dough away. Give it a one-quarter turn. Repeat process rhythmically until the dough is smooth and elastic, 5 to 8 min., using as little additional flour as possible. Always turn the dough in the same direction.

RISING—When dough looks double its original size, test by gently pressing two finges into the dough; if dent remains, dough has doubled and is light. Punch down doubled dough with fist; pull edges in to center and turn dough completely over in bowl. Dough is either allowed to rise again or it is shaped.

SHAPING LOAVES—Form dough into a smooth round ball and with a sharp knife, cut dough into halves. With fingers flatten one half of the dough and form it into a 9 x 7 x 1-in. oblong. The width should be about the same as the length of bread pan. Fold narrow ends to center of oblong, overlapping slightly. Press each end down firmly; shape evenly. Seal dough into shape by pinching center fold and ends. Round top of loaf and place sealed edge down, in prepared pan. Repeat for other half of dough. Cover loaves and let rise until doubled.

LOAVES

Basic White Bread

ONE 2-POUND LOAF
OR TWO
1-POUND LOAVES

5½ to 6 cups flour
2 packages active dry yeast
2 tablespoons sugar
2 teaspoons salt
1 cup milk
1 cup water
2 tablespoons oil
Oil or butter

QUICK MIX METHOD

1. Combine 2 cups flour, yeast, sugar, and salt in a large mixing bowl.
2. Heat milk, water, and 2 tablespoons oil in a saucepan over low heat until very warm (120° to 130°F).
3. Add liquid to flour mixture; beat on high speed of electric mixer until smooth, about 3 minutes. Gradually stir in more flour to make a soft dough.
4. Turn onto lightly floured surface and knead until smooth and elastic (5 to 10 minutes).
5. Cover dough with bowl or pan; let rest 20 minutes.
6. For two loaves, divide dough in half and roll out two 14x7-inch rectangles; for one loaf roll out to 16x8-inch rectangle.
7. Roll up from narrow side, pressing dough into roll at each turn. Press ends to seal and fold under loaf.
8. Place in 2 greased 8x4x2-inch loaf pans or 1 greased 9x5x3-inch loaf pan; brush with oil.
9. Let rise in warm place until double in bulk (30 to 45 minutes).
10. Bake at 400°F 35 to 40 minutes.
11. Remove from pans immediately and brush with oil; cool on wire rack.

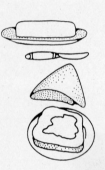

CONVENTIONAL METHOD

1. Heat milk, sugar, oil, and salt; cool to lukewarm.
2. In a large bowl, sprinkle yeast in warm water (105° to 115°F); stir until dissolved.
3. Add lukewarm milk mixture and 2 cups flour; beat until smooth.
4. Beat in enough additional flour to make a stiff dough.
5. Turn out onto lightly floured surface; let rest 10 to 15 minutes. Knead until smooth and elastic (8 to 10 minutes).
6. Place in a greased bowl, turning to grease top. Cover; let rise in warm place until double in bulk (about 1 hour).
7. Punch down. Let rest 15 minutes.
8. Follow same shaping and baking instructions as Quick Mix Method.

You'll want to try these flavor variations to the Basic White Bread for something different. Shaping variations are also included.

Cheese Bread: Add **1 cup (4 ounces) shredded Cheddar cheese** before the last portion of the flour.

Onion Bread: Omit the salt and add **1 package (1⅜ ounces) dry onion soup mix** to the warm milk.

Mini Loaves: Divide dough into 10 equal pieces. Shape into loaves. Place in 10 greased 4½x2½x1½-inch loaf pans. Cover; let rise until double in bulk (about 20 minutes). Bake at 350°F 20 to 25 minutes.

(continued)

Basic White Bread

Braided Egg Bread: Reduce milk to ½ cup. Add **2 eggs** with warm liquid to the flour mixture. Divide dough into 3 equal pieces. Form each into a rope, 15x12 inches. Braid. Tuck ends under. Place on a greased baking sheet or 9x5x3-inch loaf pan. Cover and let rise and bake the same as basic recipe.

French Bread: Omit the milk and oil and use **2 cups water.** Divide dough in half. Roll each half into 15x12-inch rectangle. Beginning at long side, roll up tightly. Seal seams. Taper the ends. With a sharp knife, make ¼-inch deep diagonal cuts along loaf tops. Cover. Let rise until less than double in bulk (about 20 minutes). Brush with water. Bake at 400°F 15 minutes, then reduce to 350°F and bake 15 to 20 minutes longer. For crisper crust, put pan of hot water in bottom of oven and 5 minutes before loaf is done, brush with glaze of **1 beaten egg white** and **1 tablespoon cold water.**

Delicatessen Rye Bread

2 LOAVES

2 to 2¾ cups all-purpose or unbleached flour
2 cups rye flour
2 teaspoons salt
2 packages active dry yeast
1 tablespoon caraway seed
1 cup milk
¾ cup water
2 tablespoons molasses
2 tablespoons oil

1. Combine 1¾ cups all-purpose flour, salt, yeast, and caraway seed in a large mixing bowl.
2. Heat milk, water, molasses, and oil in a saucepan over low heat until very warm (120° to 130°F).
3. Add liquid gradually to flour mixture, beating on high speed of electric mixer; scrape bowl occasionally. Add 1 cup rye flour, or enough to make a thick batter. Beat at high speed 2 minutes. Stir in remaining rye flour and enough all-purpose flour to make a soft dough.
4. Turn dough onto a floured surface; knead until smooth and elastic (about 5 minutes).
5. Cover with bowl or pan and let rest 20 minutes.
6. Divide in half. Shape into 2 round loaves; place on greased baking sheets. Cover; let rise until double in bulk (30 to 45 minutes).
7. Bake at 375°F 35 to 40 minutes, or until done.

Dark Rye Bread

2 LARGE LOAVES

2 cups milk, scalded
2 tablespoons butter
2 tablespoons sugar
1 teaspoon salt
1 package active dry yeast
½ cup lukewarm water
4 cup rye flour
2½ cups whole-wheat flour
2 tablespoons caraway seed

1. Pour scalded milk over butter, sugar, and salt in a large bowl; stir. Cool.
2. Dissolve yeast in lukewarm water.
3. Add softened yeast and 3 cups rye flour to milk mixture. Beat thoroughly, then beat in remaining rye flour.
4. Cover and let rise in warm place until doubled in bulk. Turn onto well-floured surface. Knead in whole-wheat flour and caraway seed. Knead until dough is smooth.
5. Divide dough in half and shape into 2 round or oblong loaves. Place round loaves in greased round pans; oblong loaves in greased loaf pans. Cover and let rise in warm place until doubled in bulk.
6. Bake at 450°F 15 minutes; reduce heat to 350°F and bake 35 to 40 minutes longer. Brush with melted butter 5 minutes before done if a more tender crust is desired.

Whole Wheat Bread

2 LOAVES

¼ cup warm water (105°F for dry yeast, 95°F for compressed yeast)
1 package yeast, active dry or compressed
1½ cups scalded milk, cooled to 105° or 95°F
1 cup honey
2 tablespoons olive oil
2 tablespoons salt
6 to 6½ cups whole wheat flour

1. Pour water into a bowl; add yeast and stir until dissolved. Add milk, honey, olive oil, and salt. Stir with a wooden spoon until well blended.
2. Stir in 4 cups of flour, 1 cup at a time. Beat until dough is smooth and elastic. Mix in another cup of flour. The dough will be very stiff.
3. Measure another cup of flour; sprinkle half of it on a board. Turn dough onto the board. Knead dough, adding flour to board until the dough no longer sticks. Continue kneading until dough is not sticky (about 8 minutes).
4. Put dough into a greased bowl about three times the size of the dough. Turn dough to grease surface lightly. Cover bowl with a towel and let rise in a warm place for about 2 hours, or until double in bulk. Test by inserting a finger about ½ inch into dough. If indentation remains, the dough is ready to shape.
5. Punch dough down; squeeze out air bubbles and shape into a smooth ball. Let rise again in warm place for about 30 minutes.
6. Divide into equal portions for 2 loaves. Form each into a smooth oval loaf. Let stand covered for 15 minutes.
7. Place the loaves seam side down in 2 greased 9x5x3-inch loaf pans. Cover with a towel and let rise in warm place until almost double in bulk (about 1 hour).
8. Bake at 375°F about 30 minutes, or until crust is medium brown.
9. Turn out of pans at once. Cool on wire racks.

Whole Wheat-Oatmeal Bread

2 LARGE LOAVES
OR 8
MINIATURE
LOAVES

2¼ cups milk
¼ cup butter or margarine
1 tablespoon salt
¼ cup firmly packed brown sugar
2½ to 2¾ cups all-purpose flour
2 cups whole wheat flour
2 packages active dry yeast
2 cups uncooked oats
⅔ cup wheat germ

1. Heat milk, butter, salt, and sugar in a saucepan until lukewarm. Pour liquid into a large mixer bowl. Add 1 cup all-purpose flour and 1 cup whole wheat flour; beat 2 minutes at medium speed of electric mixer. Add remaining whole wheat flour and yeast; beat 2 minutes at medium speed. Stir in oats, wheat germ, and enough additional all-purpose flour to make a soft dough.
2. Turn dough onto a floured surface; knead until smooth and elastic (about 10 minutes). Round dough into a ball. Place in a greased bowl; lightly grease surface of dough. Cover; let rise in a warm place until nearly double in bulk (about 1 hour).
3. Punch dough down; shape into 2 large or 8 miniature loaves. Place in greased 8x4x2½-inch or 4x3x2-inch loaf pans. Let rise in a warm place until nearly double in bulk.
4. Bake at 375°F 45 minutes for large loaves or 30 minutes for miniature loaves. Remove from pans immediately; cool on wire rack.

Freezer Oatmeal Bread

4 LOAVES

12 to 13 cups all-purpose
  flour
4 packages active dry yeast
2 tablespoons salt
2 cups milk
2 cups water
½ cup honey
¼ cup vegetable oil
2 cups uncooked oats
½ cup wheat germ
Oil

1. Combine 2 cups flour, yeast, and salt in a large mixing bowl.
2. Heat milk, water, honey, and oil in a saucepan until very warm (120° to 130°F).
3. Add the liquid gradually to flour mixture, beating 3 minutes on high speed of electric mixer until smooth. Stir in oats, wheat germ, and enough remaining flour to make a soft dough.
4. Turn dough onto a floured surface; knead until smooth and elastic (8 to 10 minutes).
5. Divide dough into quarters. Shape each quarter into a loaf, and either place in an 8x4x2-inch loaf pan or on a baking sheet. Freeze just until firm. Remove from pan. Wrap tightly in aluminum foil or freezer wrap. Dough will keep up to 2 weeks.
6. To bake, remove wrapping and place dough in a greased 8x4x2-inch loaf pan. Thaw in refrigerator overnight or at room temperature 2 hours. Brush with oil and let rise in a warm place until double in bulk (about 2 hours).
7. Bake at 400°F 30 to 35 minutes, or until done.

Freezer Whole Wheat Bread: Follow recipe for Freezer Oatmeal Bread, substituting **5 cups whole wheat flour** for 5 cups all-purpose flour.

Freezer White Bread: Follow recipe for Freezer Oatmeal Bread, omitting oats and wheat germ and increasing flour by about 1 cup.

Church Bread

1 LOAF

1 package active dry yeast
2½ cups warm water (105°
  to 115°)
6 cups all-purpose flour
1 teaspoon salt
Prosphoron seal

1. Sprinkle yeast over ¼ cup warm water; stir until dissolved.
2. Combine 5½ cups of flour and salt in a large bowl and make a well in the center. Pour in yeast and remaining warm water. Mix with a wooden spoon.
3. Sprinkle remaining flour over a board. Knead 10 minutes, adding as little flour as possible to the board. Dough will be sticky.
4. Put dough into a large bowl, cover with a cloth, and let rise in a warm place until double in bulk.
5. Sprinkle board with a little flour, punch dough down, and knead 15 minutes. (Dough should be firm and smooth.)
6. Form into a large round loaf and place in a heavily floured 12-inch round pan. Lightly flour the top of the loaf. Flour the phosphoron seal. Press seal down firmly in the center to make a sharp impression and leave on the dough.
7. Cover and allow to rise in a warm place until double in bulk. Remove seal.
8. Bake at 350°F for 1 hour. Remove from pan to cool.

Peasant Black Bread

3½ cups rye flour
½ cup unsweetened cocoa
¼ cup sugar
3 tablespoons caraway seed
2 packages active dry yeast
1 tablespoon instant coffee
(powder or crystals)
2 teaspoons salt
2½ cups hot water (120°-130°F)
¼ cup vinegar
¼ cup dark molasses
¼ cup vegetable oil or
melted butter
3½ to 4½ cups unbleached
or all-purpose flour

1. Thoroughly mix rye flour, cocoa, sugar, caraway, yeast, coffee, and salt in a large mixing bowl.
2. Stir in water, vinegar, molasses, and oil; beat until smooth.
3. Stir in enough unbleached flour to make a soft dough.
4. Turn onto a floured surface. Knead until smooth and elastic (about 5 minutes).
5. Place in an oiled bowl; turn to oil top of dough. Cover; let rise in warm place until doubled (about 1 hour).
6. Punch dough down. Divide in half; shape each half into a ball and place in center of 2 greased 8-inch round cake pans. Cover; let rise until double in bulk (about 1 hour).
7. Bake at 350°F 40 to 45 minutes, or until done.
2 LOAVES

Ground Nut Bread

2 LOAVES

3 cups all-purpose flour
1½ cups whole wheat flour
2 packages active dry yeast
2 teaspoons salt
1¾ cups hot tap water (120°
to 130°F)
¼ cup honey
2 tablespoons vegetable oil
1 cup rolled oats
1 cup ground unsalted nuts
½ cup ground unsalted
hulled sunflower seeds
½ cup cornmeal

1. Mix flours.
2. Combine 1¾ cups flour mixture, yeast, and salt in a large mixing bowl.
3. Add water, honey, and oil to flour mixture; beat until smooth, about 3 minutes on high speed of electric mixer.
4. Stir in oats, nuts, sunflower seeds, cornmeal, and enough more flour to make a soft dough.
5. Turn dough onto a floured board; knead until smooth and elastic (5 to 8 minutes).
6. Place in an oiled bowl; turn to oil top of dough. Cover; let rise in a warm place until double in bulk (about 1 hour).
7. Punch dough down. Divide in half, then each half in thirds. Form each piece into a rope 12 to 15 inches long. For each loaf, braid 3 pieces together. Tuck ends under; place in 2 greased 9x5x3-inch loaf pans or on greased baking sheets. Cover; let rise until double in bulk (about 1 hour).
8. Bake at 375°F 35 to 40 minutes, or until done.

Italian Bread

2 LOAVES

1 package active dry yeast
2 cups warm water
1 tablespoon salt
5 to 5½ cups sifted all-
  purpose flour

1. Soften yeast in ¼ cup warm water. Set aside.
2. Combine remaining 1¾ cups water and salt in a large bowl. Blend in 3 cups flour. Stir softened yeast and add to flour mixture, mixing well.
3. Add about half the remaining flour to the yeast mixture and beat until very smooth. Mix in enough remaining flour to make a soft dough. Turn dough onto lightly floured surface. Allow to rest 5 to 10 minutes. Knead 5 to 8 minutes, until dough is smooth and elastic.
4. Shape dough into a smooth ball and place in a greased bowl, just large enough to allow dough to double. Turn dough to bring greased surface to the top. Cover bowl with waxed paper and a towel. Let stand in warm place (about 80°F) until dough is doubled (1½ to 2 hours).
5. When dough has doubled in bulk, punch down with fist. Knead on a lightly floured surface about 2 minutes. Divide into 2 equal balls. Cover with towel and let stand 10 minutes.
6. Roll each ball into a 14x8-inch rectangle. Roll up lightly from wide side into a long, slender loaf. Pinch ends to seal. Place loaves on a lightly greased 15x10-inch baking sheet. Cover loaves loosely with a towel and set aside in a warm place until doubled.
7. Bake at 425°F 10 minutes. Turn oven control to 350°F and bake 1 hour, or until golden brown.

Note: To increase crustiness, place shallow pan on the bottom of the oven and fill with boiling water at the beginning of the baking time.

Colonial Bread

2 LOAVES

2 cups whole wheat flour
2½ cups unbleached or all-
  purpose flour
¾ cup rye flour
½ cup yellow cornmeal
⅓ cup firmly packed brown
  sugar
2 packages active dry yeast
1 tablespoon salt
2½ cups hot tap water (120°
  to 130°F)
¼ cup vegetable oil
1 egg

1. Blend flours and cornmeal. Combine 2½ cups flour mixture, sugar, yeast, and salt in a large mixing bowl.
2. Stir water, oil, and egg into flour mixture; beat until smooth, about 3 minutes on high speed of electric mixer.
3. Gradually stir in enough more flour mixture to make a soft dough.
4. Turn dough onto a floured surface; knead until smooth and elastic (5 to 8 minutes).
5. Place in an oiled bowl; turn to oil top of dough. Cover; let rise in a warm place until double in bulk (about 1 hour).
6. Punch dough down. Divide in half; shape into loaves. Place in 2 greased 9x5x3-inch loaf pans. Cover; let rise until double in bulk (about 30 minutes).
7. Bake at 375°F 35 to 40 minutes, or until done.

Hearty Potato Bread

2 LOAVES

6½ to 7½ cups flour
2 packages active dry yeast
2 tablespoons sugar
1 tablespoon salt
2¼ cups hot potato water
1 cup warm unseasoned
  mashed potatoes
2 tablespoons oil

1. Combine flour, yeast, sugar, and salt in a large mixing bowl.
2. Add potato water (see Note), potatoes, and oil to flour mixture; beat about 3 minutes on high speed of electric mixer.
3. Stir in enough more flour to make a soft dough.

4. Turn dough onto a floured surface; knead until smooth and elastic (5 to 8 minutes).
5. Place in an oiled bowl; turn to oil top of dough. Cover; let rise in a warm place until double in bulk (about 1 hour).
6. Punch dough down. Divide in half; shape into loaves and place in 2 greased 9x5x3-inch loaf pans. Cover; let rise until double in bulk (about 45 minutes).
7. Bake at 375°F 40 to 45 minutes, or until done.

Note: To make potato water, cook 2 pared, cut-up potatoes until tender in about 3 cups water. Drain, reserving water. Mash potatoes and cool for bread.

Mushroom Bread

4 MUSHROOMS OR 2 ROUND LOAVES

¼ cup margarine
½ pound mushrooms, finely chopped
1 cup finely chopped onion
2 cups milk
3 tablespoons molasses
4 teaspoons salt
¼ teaspoon pepper
½ cup warm water (105° to 115°F)
2 packages active dry yeast
1 egg
1 cup wheat germ
8 to 9 cups all-purpose flour

1. Melt 2 tablespoons margarine in a large skillet over medium heat. Add mushrooms and onion; sauté until onion is tender and liquid has evaporated. Cool.
2. Heat milk; stir in molasses, salt, and pepper. Cool to lukewarm.
3. Measure warm water into a large warm bowl. Sprinkle in yeast; stir until dissolved. Add lukewarm milk mixture, egg, wheat germ, and 2 cups flour; beat until smooth. Stir in enough additional flour to make a stiff dough.
4. Turn dough onto a lightly floured surface; knead until smooth and elastic (8 to 10 minutes). Place in a greased bowl; turn to grease top. Cover; let rise in a warm place until double in bulk (about 1 hour).
5. Meanwhile, use four 30-ounce fruit cans to prepare Mushroom Pans (see below).
6. Punch dough down; turn onto lightly floured surface.

To Make Mushrooms: Divide dough onto 4 equal pieces. Shape each piece into a smooth round ball. Place in prepared Mushroom Pans. Let rise in a warm place until double in bulk (about 1 hour). With fingertips, gently press lower edge of mushroom cap down to meet foil-covered collar. Reshape cap if necessary. If desired, brush mushrooms with a mixture of 1 egg beaten with 1 tablespoon water. Bake on lowest rack position at 400°F about 40 minutes, or until done. Carefully remove from pans and cool on wire racks.

To Make Loaves: Divide dough in half. Roll each half to a 14x9-inch rectangle. Shape into loaves. Place in 2 greased 9x5x3-inch loaf pans. Cover; let rise in a warm place until double in bulk (about 1 hour). Bake at 400°F about 45 minutes, or until done. Remove from pans and cool on wire racks.

Mushroom Pans: Cut 4 heavy cardboard squares 2 inches wider than can opening. Trace can opening in center of squares and cut out. Cover rings with foil. Place rings over cans so they fit tightly around opening. Grease cans and foil collars well.

Harvest Bread

Harvest Bread

2 LOAVES OR 1 SHEAF

1½ cups milk
⅓ cup margarine
2 tablespoons honey
2 tablespoons light molasses
2 teaspoons salt
2 large shredded wheat biscuits, crumbled
½ cup warm water (105° to 115°F)
2 packages active dry yeast
2 cups whole wheat flour
¼ cup wheat germ
2 to 3 cups all-purpose flour

1. Heat milk; stir in margarine, honey, molasses, salt, and shredded wheat biscuits. Cool to lukewarm.
2. Measure warm water into a large warm bowl. Sprinkle in yeast; stir until dissolved. Add lukewarm milk mixture and whole wheat flour; beat until smooth. Stir in wheat germ and enough all-purpose flour to make a stiff dough.
3. Turn dough onto a lightly floured surface; knead until smooth and elastic (8 to 10 minutes). Place in a greased bowl; turn to grease top. Cover; let rise in a warm place until double in bulk (about 1 hour).
4. Punch dough down; divide in half. Proceed, following directions below for desired shape.
5. Cover; let rise in a warm place until double in bulk (about 1 hour). If making sheaf, make diagonal snips with scissors along the bent portion of stalks above the twist. If desired, gently brush sheaf with beaten egg.
6. Bake on lowest rack position at 400°F about 20 minutes for sheaves and 25 to 30 minutes for loaves, or until done. Remove from baking sheets and cool on wire racks.

To make round loaves: Shape each half of dough into

a smooth round ball. Press each ball slightly to flatten into rounds 6 inches in diameter. Place on greased baking sheets.

To Make Wheat Sheaf: Divide one half of dough into 18 equal pieces. Roll 2 pieces into 12-inch ropes. Twist ropes together; set aside. Roll 8 pieces into 18-inch ropes and roll remaining 8 pieces into 15-inch ropes. Place one 18-inch rope lengthwise on center of a greased baking sheet, bending top third of rope off to the left at a 45-degree angle. Place a second 18-inch rope on sheet touching the first rope but bending top third off to the right. Repeat procedure using two more 18-inch ropes, placing them along outer edges of straight section and inside bent sections so that ropes are touching. Repeat, using two of the 15-inch ropes. Repeat, starting with the long ropes, placing them on top of the arranged long ropes and slightly spreading out ropes forming bottom of sheaf. Fill in by topping with the remaining 15-inch ropes, making shorter bends in two uppermost ropes. Cut twist in half. Arrange twists side by side around center of sheaf, tuck ends underneath. Repeat with remaining half of dough.

Anadama Batter Bread

1 LOAF

1 package active dry yeast
¼ cup warm water
1 cup cornmeal
2 teaspoons salt
½ teaspoon baking soda
⅓ cup dark molasses
3 tablespoons shortening
¾ cup boiling water
1 egg
2¼ cups all-purpose flour
Melted butter

1. Dissolve yeast in warm water.
2. Combine cornmeal, salt, baking soda, molasses, and shortening in a large mixer bowl. Stir in boiling water; cool to lukewarm.
3. Add softened yeast, egg, and 1 cup flour to cornmeal mixture; beat 2 minutes on medium speed of electric mixer or 300 vigorous strokes with a wooden spoon. Stir in remaining flour.
4. Spread batter in a well-greased 2-quart casserole. Cover; let rise in a warm place until nearly double in bulk (1 to 1½ hours).
5. Bake at 350°F about 40 minutes. Remove from casserole immediately. Brush top lightly with melted butter; cool.

Anadama Batter Bread

Greek Sesame Bread

TWO 9-INCH
ROUND LOAVES

2 packages active dry yeast
1 cup lukewarm water
1 cup milk, scalded
3 tablespoons sugar
1 tablespoon salt
4 tablespoons butter, cut in pieces
1 egg
5½ to 6 cups flour
Cornmeal
2 tablespoons half-and-half
3 tablespoons sesame seed

1. Add yeast to lukewarm water and stir until dissolved.
2. In a 1-quart measuring cup, combine scalded milk, sugar, salt, and butter and stir until dissolved. Cool to lukewarm.
3. Using **steel blade** of food processor, lightly beat egg. Add egg and yeast mixture to cooled milk mixture.
4. Aside, measure half of flour (3 cups flour). Using **steel blade,** put 2 cups of flour into the bowl and add half of liquid ingredients. Process a few seconds until thoroughly blended. Add remaining cup of flour, ¼ cup at a time, until dough forms into a slightly sticky, smooth ball around edge of bowl, usually after 2½ to 2¾ cups flour. Let ball of dough spin around bowl for 20 to 30 seconds to knead the dough. Turn ball of dough onto floured board, knead for a minute by hand, and form into a neat ball.
5. Transfer dough to a greased bowl and rotate to coat all sides. Cover with a towel and place in a warm, draft-free place to rise for 1½ to 2 hours, or until double in bulk.
6. Repeat procedure, using remaining flour and liquid ingredients. Combine two balls of dough only if making one large loaf.
7. When double in bulk, punch down and turn dough onto lightly floured board; form into ball again. Place each ball of dough into a well-greased 9-inch round cake pan, lightly sprinkled with cornmeal.
8. Brush each loaf with half-and-half and sprinkle with sesame seed. Cover and put into a warm, draft-free place to rise for 1½ to 2 hours.
9. Bake at 350°F for 40 minutes, or until loaves are crusty.

Greek Sesame Bread

Carrot Brown Bread

2 LOAVES

3 cups whole wheat flour
4 cups unbleached or all-purpose flour
2 packages active dry yeast
2 teaspoons salt
2 cups milk
½ cup water
¼ cup vegetable oil
2 tablespoons honey
2 tablespoons molasses
1 cup grated carrot

1. Mix flours.
2. Combine 2 cups flour mixture, yeast, and salt in a large mixing bowl.
3. Heat milk, water, oil, honey, and molasses in a saucepan until very warm (120° to 130°F).
4. Add liquid gradually to flour mixture, beating 3 minutes on high speed of electric mixer.
5. Stir in carrot and enough more flour to make a soft dough.
6. Turn dough onto a floured surface; allow to rest 10 minutes for easier handling. Knead until smooth and elastic (5 to 8 minutes).
7. Place dough in an oiled bowl; turn to oil top of dough. Cover; let rise in a warm place until double in bulk (about 1 hour).
8. Punch dough down; divide in half. Either shape into 2 round loaves and place on a greased baking sheet, or shape into 2 loaves and place in 2 greased 9 x 5 x 3-inch loaf pans. Cover; let rise until double in bulk (about 30 minutes).
9. Bake at 375°F 40 to 45 minutes, or until done.

Piquant Cheese Loaf

2 LOAVES
BREAD

7 to 7½ cups sifted enriched
all-purpose flour
1 teaspoon sugar
1 tablespoon salt
2 packages active dry yeast
1 cup plain yogurt
½ cup water
2 tablespoons margarine
6 eggs (at room temperature)
½ pound muenster cheese,
shredded (about 2 cups)
2 cups julienne cooked ham
(optional)
1 egg, slightly beaten
1 tablespoon milk

1. Mix 1½ cups flour, sugar, salt, and undissolved yeast thoroughly in a larger mixer bowl.

2. Combine yogurt, water, and margarine in a saucepan. Set over low heat until very warm (120-130°F); margarine does not need to melt. Add liquid mixture gradually to dry ingredients while beating at low speed of electric mixer. Beat at medium speed 2 minutes, scraping bowl occasionally. Add 6 eggs, 1 cup flour, and 1½ cups shredded cheese. Beat at high speed 2 minutes, scraping bowl occasionally. Stir in enough of the remaining flour to make a stiff dough.

3. Turn dough onto a lightly floured surface. Knead 8 to 10 minutes, or until dough is smooth, elastic, and shows small blisters under surface when drawn tight.

4. Form dough into a ball and place in greased deep bowl; turn to bring greased surface to top. Cover; let rise in a warm place until double in bulk (about 1 hour).

5. Punch down dough; turn onto lightly floured surface. Divide in half. If using ham, knead 1 cup ham strips into each half. Shape each half into a ball and place on a greased cookie sheet. Cover; let rise again until double in bulk (about 1 hour).

6. Combine eggs and milk; brush over loaves. Sprinkle with remaining ½ cup cheese.

7. Bake at 350°F about 30 minutes. Remove from cookie sheets and place on wire racks to cool.

Mozzarella Egg Bread

2 LOAVES

7 to 8 cups all-purpose flour
2 packages active dry yeast
1 tablespoon sugar
1 tablespoon salt
6 eggs (at room temperature)
1 cup plain yogurt
2 cups shredded mozzarella cheese (8 ounces)
½ cup hot water (120° to 130°F)

1. Combine 2 cups flour, yeast, sugar, and salt in a mixing bowl.
2. Stir eggs, yogurt, 1½ cups cheese, and water into flour mixture; beat until smooth, about 3 minutes on high speed of electric mixer.
3. Stir in enough more flour to make a soft dough.
4. Turn dough onto a floured surface; knead until smooth and elastic (5 to 8 minutes).
5. Place in an oiled bowl; turn to oil top of dough. Cover; let rise in a warm place until double in bulk (about 1 hour).
6. Punch dough down. Divide in half; shape into loaves, and place in 2 greased 9x5x3-inch loaf pans. Cover; let rise until double, about 30 minutes. Top loaves with remaining cheese.
7. Bake at 375°F 30 minutes, or until done.

Oregano and Kefalotyri Cheese Bread

1 LOAF

3 to 3½ cups all-purpose flour
2 tablespoons sugar
1½ teaspoons salt
2 packages active dry yeast
¾ cup milk
¼ cup water
¼ cup shortening
1 egg
3 tablespoons oregano
¼ teaspoon garlic powder
½ cup grated kefalotyri cheese
1 teaspoon mint
2 tablespoons basil
¼ cup instant minced onion
1 tablespoon sesame seed

1. Combine 1 cup flour, sugar, salt, and dry yeast in a large bowl.
2. Heat milk, water, and shortening in a saucepan until warm. (Shortening will not melt completely.) Add milk mixture and egg to flour mixture. Beat until smooth.
3. Mix oregano, garlic powder, cheese, mint, basil, onion, and sesame seed. Stir into dough. Gradually add more flour to form a stiff dough.
4. Turn into a greased loaf pan. Cover with a towel. Let rise in a warm place until double in bulk (about 1 hour).
5. Bake at 350° about 40 minutes, or until golden brown.

Triple Treat Bread

2 LOAVES

4½ cups all-purpose or unbleached flour
2 cups whole wheat flour
1 cup rye flour
½ cup firmly packed brown sugar
½ cup instant nonfat dry milk
2 packages active dry yeast
1 tablespoon salt
2 cups hot tap water (120° to 130°F)
¼ cup vegetable oil

1. Mix flours.
2. Combine 2 cups flour mixture, sugar, dry milk, yeast, and salt in a large mixing bowl.
3. Stir water and oil into flour mixture; beat until smooth, about 3 minutes on high speed of electric mixer. Stir in enough remaining flour to make a soft dough.
4. Turn dough onto a floured surface; knead until smooth and elastic (5 to 8 minutes).
5. Place in an oiled bowl; turn to oil top of dough. Cover; let rise in a warm place until double (about 45 minutes).
6. Punch dough down. Divide in half; shape into loaves and place in 2 greased 9x5x3-inch loaf pans. Cover; let rise until double in bulk (about 30 minutes).
7. Bake at 375°F 35 to 40 minutes, or until done.

Mozzarella Egg Bread

Here's-To-Your-Health Bread

3 LOAVES

4½ cups all-purpose or
  unbleached flour
3 cups whole wheat flour
1 cup uncooked oats
½ cup wheat germ
2 packages active dry yeast
2 teaspoons salt
2½ cups hot tap water (120°
  to 130°F)
1½ cups (12 ounces)
  creamed cottage cheese (at
  room temperature)
½ cup molasses or honey
2 tablespoons vegetable oil
1 cup raisins

1. Mix flours and oats.
2. Combine 3 cups flour mixture, wheat germ, yeast, and salt in a large mixing bowl.
3. Add water, cottage cheese, molasses, and oil to flour mixture; beat until smooth, about 3 minutes on high speed of electric mixer.
4. Stir in raisins and enough more flour to make a soft dough.
5. Turn dough onto a floured surface; let rest 10 minutes for easier handling. Knead until smooth and elastic (5 to 8 minutes).
6. Place in an oiled bowl; turn dough to oil top. Cover; let rise in a warm place until double in bulk (about 1 hour).
7. Punch dough down. Divide dough in thirds; shape into loaves and place in 3 greased 9x5x3-inch loaf pans. Cover; let rise until double in bulk (about 30 minutes).
8. Bake at 375°F 30 to 35 minutes, or until done.

Cornmeal French Bread

1 LARGE LOAF

1 cup cooked cornmeal mush
  (see recipe below)
2 packages active dry yeast
½ cup warm water
1 cup milk, scalded
1 tablespoon sugar
2½ teaspoons salt
4¾ to 5¼ cups all-purpose
  flour

1. Prepare cornmeal mush; cool slightly.
2. Dissolve yeast in warm water.
3. Pour scalded milk over sugar and salt in a large bowl. Add mush and mix well; cool to lukewarm. Beat in 1 cup flour. Mix in yeast and enough additional flour to make a soft dough.
4. Turn dough onto a lightly floured surface. Knead until smooth and satiny (about 10 minutes).
5. Put dough into a greased bowl; turn to grease top. Cover; let rise in a warm place until double in bulk (about 1 hour).
6. Punch dough down; cover and let rest 10 minutes. Form into a long thin roll on greased baking sheet. With a sharp knife, cut diagonal ¼-inch-deep slits about 2½ inches apart across the top. Brush top of loaf with salt water (**1 tablespoon salt** dissolved in **¼ cup water**). Cover; let rise until double in bulk (about 45 minutes).
7. Pour boiling water into a pie pan to a ½-inch depth; set on bottom rack of oven.
8. Bake at 400°F 15 minutes; turn temperature control to 350°F and bake 30 to 35 minutes longer. About 5 minutes before bread is finished baking, baste with salt water.

Cornmeal Mush: Heat **3 cups water** to boiling in a saucepan. Mix **1 cup cornmeal, 1 teaspoon salt,** and **1 cup cold water.** Pour cornmeal mixture into boiling water, stirring constantly. Cook until thickened, stirring frequently. Cover; continue cooking over low heat 10 minutes.
4 CUPS

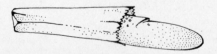

ROLLS

Basic Dinner Rolls

**2 TO 2½
DOZEN ROLLS**

**4 to 4¾ cups all-purpose
  flour**
2 tablespoons sugar
2 packages active dry yeast
1 teaspoon salt
1 cup milk
½ cup water
¼ cup butter or margarine
1 egg (at room temperature)
Melted butter (optional)

1. Combine 1½ cups flour, sugar, yeast, and salt in a mixing bowl.
2. Heat milk, water, and butter until very warm (120° to 130°F).
3. Add liquid and egg to flour mixture; beat until smooth, about 3 minutes.
4. Stir in enough remaining flour to make a soft, sticky dough.
5. Turn dough onto a floured surface; continue to work in flour until dough can be kneaded. Knead until smooth and elastic, but still soft (about 5 minutes).
6. Cover dough with bowl or pan. Let rest 20 minutes.
7. Shape dough as desired. Cover and let rise until double in bulk (about 15 minutes).
8. Bake at 425°F about 12 minutes. Cool on wire rack. Brush with butter if desired.

Pan Rolls: Divide dough into 24 equal pieces by first dividing dough in half and then each half into 12 equal pieces. Roll into balls. Place in a greased 13x9x2-inch baking pan. Brush with melted butter, if desired.

Cloverleaf Rolls: Pinch off bits of dough; roll into 1-inch balls. For each roll, place 3 balls in a greased muffin-pan well.

Crescents: Divide dough in half. Roll each half into a 12-inch round about ¼ inch thick. Brush with **2 tablespoons melted butter.** Cut into 12 wedges. For each crescent, roll up wedge beginning at side opposite the point. Place point-side down on a greased baking sheet; curve ends.

Snails: Roll dough into a rectangle ¼ inch thick. Cut off strips ½ inch wide and 5 inches long. Roll each piece of dough into a rope about 10 inches long. Wind into a flat coil, tucking ends under. Place on greased baking sheet.

Figure Eights: Shape strips of dough ½ inch wide and 5 inches long into 10-inch ropes as in Snails (above). For each roll, pinch ends of rope together and twist once to form a figure 8. Place on greased baking sheets.

Twists: Follow procedure for Figure Eights, giving each 8 an additional twist.

Bowknots: Roll dough into a rectangle ¼ inch thick. Cut off strips ½ inch wide and 5 inches long. Roll each strip into a smooth rope 9 or 10 inches long. Gently tie into a single or double knot. Place on a greased baking sheet.

Parker House Rolls: Roll dough ¼ inch thick. Brush with

(continued)

Basic Dinner Rolls

3 or 4 tablespoons melted butter. Cut with a 2½-inch round cutter. With a knife handle, make a crease across each circle slightly off center. Fold larger half over the smaller, pressing edges to seal. Place on a greased baking sheet or close together in a greased 13x9x2-inch baking pan.

Braids: Form several ropes, ½ inch in diameter. Braid 3 ropes into a long strip; cut into 3-inch strips. Pinch together at each end. Place on a greased baking sheet.

Butterflies: Divide dough in half. Roll each half into a 24x6-inch rectangle about ¼ inch thick. Brush with 2 **tablespoons melted butter.** Starting with long side, roll up dough as for jelly roll. Cut off 2-inch pieces. With handle of knife, press crosswise at center of each roll, forming a deep groove so spiral sides become visible. Place on a greased baking sheet.

Fantans or Butterflake Rolls: Roll dough into a rectangle ¼ inch thick. Brush with **3 or 4 tablespoons melted butter.** Cut into 1-inch strips. Stack 6 or 7 strips; cut each into 1½-inch sections. Place on end in greased muffin-pan wells.

Poppy Seed Rolls

2 POPPY SEED ROLLS

Dough:
2 packages active dry yeast
½ cup warm water
4½ cups all-purpose flour
¾ cup sugar
½ teaspoon salt
½ cup butter or margarine
2 eggs
2 egg yolks
½ cup sour cream
1 teaspoon vanilla extract

Filling:
2 tablespoons butter
10 ounces poppy seed, ground twice (may be purchased already ground in gourmet shops)
2 tablespoons honey
2 teaspoons lemon juice or vanilla extract
¼ cup raisins, steamed
2 egg whites
½ cup sugar
¼ cup finely chopped candied orange peel
2 teaspoons grated lemon peel

Icing:
1 cup confectioners' sugar
2 tablespoons lemon juice

1. For dough, soften yeast in warm water in a bowl.
2. Mix flour with sugar and salt. Cut in butter with a pastry blender or two knives until mixture has a fine, even crumb.
3. Beat eggs and egg yolks; mix with yeast, then stir into flour mixture. Add sour cream and vanilla extract; mix well.
4. Knead dough on floured surface for 5 minutes. Divide in half. Roll each half of dough into a 12-inch square. Cover.
5. For filling, melt butter in a large saucepan. Add poppy seed. Stir-fry 3 minutes.
6. Add honey, lemon juice, and raisins to poppy seed. Cover and remove from heat; let stand 10 minutes.
7. Beat egg whites with sugar until stiff, not dry, peaks form. Fold in orange and lemon peels. Gently fold in poppy seed mixture.
8. Spread half of filling over each square of dough. Roll up, jelly-roll fashion. Seal edges. Place on greased baking sheets. Cover. Let rise until doubled in bulk, about 1½ hours.
9. Bake at 350°F about 45 minutes. Cool.
10. For icing, blend sugar and lemon juice until smooth. Spread over rolls.

Crusty Hard Rolls

1½ DOZEN
ROLLS

3½ to 4½ cups all-purpose
    flour
2 packages active dry yeast
1 tablespoon sugar
1½ teaspoons salt
1 cup hot tap water (120° to
    130°F)
2 tablespoons vegetable oil
1 egg white
1 egg yolk
1 tablespoon water

1. Combine 1 cup flour, yeast, sugar, and salt in a large mixer bowl. Stir in water, oil, and egg white; beat until smooth, about 3 minutes on high speed of electric mixer. Gradually stir in more flour to make a soft dough.
2. Turn dough onto a floured surface; knead until smooth and elastic (3 to 5 minutes).
3. Cover with bowl or pan and let rest about 20 minutes.
4. Divide into 18 equal pieces. Form each into a smooth oval; place on a greased baking sheet. Slash tops lengthwise about ¼ inch deep. Let rise until double in bulk (about 15 minutes).
5. Brush with a mixture of egg yolk and 1 tablespoon water.
6. Bake at 400°F 15 to 20 minutes. For a crisper crust, place a shallow pan of hot water on lowest oven rack during baking.

Kaiser Rolls: Follow recipe for Crusty Hard Rolls, only flatten each of the 18 pieces of dough into 4- to 4-½-inch rounds. For each roll, lift one edge of the round and press it into center of circle. Then lift the corner of the fold and press it into the center. Continue clockwise around the circle until 5 or 6 folds have been made. Let rise and bake as directed above.

Croissants

ABOUT
1½ DOZEN
CROISSANTS

1 cup milk
1 tablespoon oil
1 tablespoon sugar
½ teaspoon salt
1 package compressed or ac-
    tive dry yeast
¼ cup warm water (105° to
    115°F)
2¾ to 3 cups all-purpose
    flour
1 cup (½ pound) butter,
    softened
1 egg yolk
1 tablespoon milk

1. Heat 1 cup milk, oil, sugar, and salt in a saucepan; cool to lukewarm.
2. Dissolve yeast in warm water in a large bowl. Add milk mixture and 1 cup flour; beat until smooth. Stir in enough remaining flour to make a soft dough.
3. Turn dough onto a floured surface; continue to work in flour until dough can be kneaded. Knead until smooth and elastic (about 5 minutes).
4. Shape dough into a ball and place in an oiled bowl; turn to oil top of dough. Cover; let rise in a warm place until double in bulk (about 45 minutes).
5. Punch dough down. Roll out on floured surface to form a rectangle about ¼ inch thick.
6. Cut butter in slices (just soft enough to spread but not melted). Spread over center one-third section of rectangle. Fold each extending side of butter, pressing together the open edges to seal. Roll out again until rectangle is ⅜ inch thick. Turn dough occasionally, flouring surface lightly to prevent sticking. Fold in thirds again to make a squarish rectangle. Roll dough and fold again in the same manner. Wrap dough in waxed paper or foil; chill 30 minutes. If at any time dough oozes butter and becomes sticky while rolling, chill until butter is more firm.
7. Roll and fold again 2 more times exactly as directed before. Chill dough again another 30 minutes.
8. Roll dough into a rectangle about ⅛ inch thick. Cut into strips 6 inches wide. Cut triangles out of each strip to measure about 6x8x6 inches. Roll up each triangle of dough

from a 6-inch edge, pinching tip to seal. Shape each roll into a crescent. Place, point down, 1½ inches apart on ungreased baking sheet.

9. Cover; let rise until double in bulk (30 to 45 minutes).

10. Brush each roll with mixture of egg yolk and 1 tablespoon milk.

11. Bake at 425°F 15 minutes, or until brown. Remove from baking sheet and cool on wire rack. Serve warm.

Brioche (Pictured on page 35)

16 BRIOCHES

½ cup butter
⅓ cup sugar
½ teaspoon salt
½ cup undiluted evaporated milk
1 package active dry yeast
¼ cup warm water
1 egg yolk
2 eggs
3¼ cups all-purpose flour
1 egg white, unbeaten
1 tablespoon sugar

1. Cream the butter with the ⅓ cup sugar and salt in a large bowl. Beat in the evaporated milk.
2. Soften yeast in the warm water.
3. Beat egg yolk with the 2 eggs until thick and piled softly. Gradually add to the creamed mixture, beating constantly until fluffy. Blend in the yeast.
4. Add the flour, about ½ cup at a time, beating thoroughly after each addition. Cover; let rise in a warm place until doubled, about 2 hours.
5. Stir down and beat thoroughly. Cover tightly with moisture-vaporproof material and refrigerate overnight.
6. Remove from refrigerator and stir down the dough. Turn onto a lightly floured surface and divide into two portions, one using about three fourths of the dough, the other about one fourth.
7. Cut each portion into 16 equal pieces. Roll each piece into a smooth ball. Place each large ball in a well-greased muffin-pan well (2¾ x1¼ inches). Make a deep indentation with finger in center of each large ball; then moisten each depression slightly with cold water. Press a small ball into each depression.
8. Cover; let rise again until more than doubled, about 1 hour.
9. Brush tops of rolls with a mixture of the egg white and 1 tablespoon sugar.
10. Bake at 375°F about 15 minutes, or until golden brown.

Bran Rolls

2 DOZEN ROLLS

¾ cup whole bran cereal
⅓ cup sugar
1½ teaspoons salt
½ cup margarine
½ cup boiling water
½ cup warm water
2 packages active dry yeast
1 egg, beaten
3¼ to 3¾ cups sifted enriched all-purpose flour
Margarine, melted

1. Combine bran cereal, sugar, salt, and margarine in a bowl. Add boiling water; stir until margarine is melted. Cool to lukewarm.
2. Measure warm water into a warm large bowl. Sprinkle in yeast; stir until dissolved. Mix in lukewarm cereal mixture, egg, and enough of the flour to make a stiff dough.
3. Turn dough onto a lightly floured surface; knead 8 to 10 minutes, or until smooth and elastic. Form dough into a ball and place in a greased deep bowl; turn to bring greased surface to top. Cover; let rise in a warm place until double in bulk (about 1 hour).
4. Punch dough down; divide in half. Divide each half into 12 equal pieces. Form each piece into a smooth ball. Place in greased muffin-pan wells, 2½x1½ inches, or in 2 greased 8-inch round cake pans. Brush rolls with melted margarine. Cover; let rise again until double in bulk (about 30 minutes).
5. Bake at 375°F 20 to 25 minutes. Remove from pans and place on wire racks. Serve warm.

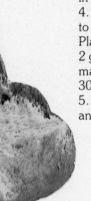

Potato Pan Rolls

Potato Pan Rolls

32 ROLLS

½ cup milk
1 tablespoon sugar
¾ teaspoon salt
2 tablespoons margarine
½ cup warm water (105° to 115°F)
1 package active dry yeast
1 egg
½ cup mashed potatoes (at room temperature)
3½ to 4½ cups all-purpose flour
Flour for dusting

1. Heat milk; stir in sugar, salt, and margarine. Cool to lukewarm.
2. Measure warm water into a large warm bowl. Sprinkle in yeast; stir until dissolved. Stir in lukewarm milk mixture, egg, mashed potatoes, and 2 cups flour. Beat until smooth. Stir in enough additional flour to make a soft dough.
3. Turn dough onto a lightly floured surface; knead until smooth and elastic (8 to 10 minutes). Place in a greased bowl; turn to grease top. Cover; let rise in a warm place until double in bulk (about 1 hour).
4. Punch dough down; turn out onto a lightly floured surface. Divide in half. Divide each half into 16 equal pieces; form into smooth balls. Place in 2 greased 9-inch round layer cake pans. Cover; let rise in a warm place until double in bulk (about 1 hour).
5. Dust rolls with flour.
6. Bake at 375°F about 25 minutes, or until done. Remove from pans and cool on wire racks.

Hurry-Up Dinner Rolls

16 ROLLS

2½ to 3 cups all-purpose flour
2 tablespoons sugar
1 package active dry yeast
½ teaspoon salt
¾ cup hot water (120° to 130°F)
1 egg (at room temperature)
2 tablespoons vegetable oil
2 tablespoons melted butter or margarine

1. Combine 1 cup flour, sugar, yeast, and salt in a bowl. Stir in water, egg, and oil; beat until smooth. Cover; let rise in a warm place 15 minutes.
2. Stir in enough remaining flour to make a soft, sticky dough.
3. Turn dough onto a floured board; continue to work in flour until dough can be kneaded. Knead until smooth and elastic (about 3 minutes).
4. Divide dough into 16 pieces; shape into balls. Place in a greased 9-inch square pan. Brush tops with melted butter. Cover; let rise 20 minutes.
5. Bake at 425°F 8 to 10 minutes.

Cloverleaf Rolls

Cloverleaf Rolls

36 ROLLS

2 packages active dry yeast
¼ cup lukewarm water
1 cup milk
8 tablespoons butter (1 stick),
   cut in 5 pieces
½ cup sugar
1 teaspoon salt
2 eggs
5 cups flour
¼ cup melted butter

1. Add yeast to lukewarm water and stir until dissolved; set aside to cool.
2. Scald milk, remove from heat, and add butter, sugar, and salt; stir to dissolve. Cool to lukewarm.
3. Using **steel blade** of food processor, beat eggs until frothy.
4. In a 1-quart measuring cup, combine yeast mixture, milk mixture, and beaten eggs and stir thoroughly.
5. Aside, measure half of flour 2½ cups). Using **steel blade,** add 2 cups flour and half of liquid ingredients; process until blended.
6. Add remaining ½ cup of flour, ¼ cup at a time, and process until dough forms itself into a fairly smooth ball. Then let ball of dough spin around the bowl for about 20 to 30 seconds to thoroughly knead the dough.
7. Turn dough onto lightly floured board, knead by hand for a minute, and form into a neat ball. Transfer to a greased bowl and rotate to coat all sides.
8. Cover with a damp cloth and place in a warm, draft-free place to rise until double in bulk (about 1½ hours).
9. Repeat procedure, using remaining ingredients.
10. When double in bulk, punch the dough down. Let it rest for 15 minutes. Break off dough and form into balls the size of a walnut.
11. Roll each ball in melted butter.
12. Grease muffin-pan wells and place 3 balls in bottom of each well.
13. Cover loosely with a towel and let rise again in a warm, draft-free place until doubled in bulk (about 1 hour).
14. Bake at 400°F about 15 minutes. Serve warm.

Brown-and-Serve Rolls

ABOUT
4 DOZEN
ROLLS

9 to 10 cups all-purpose
   flour
½ cup sugar
2 packages active dry yeast
1 tablespoon salt
2 cups warm water
1 cup milk
½ cup butter or margarine

1. Stir together 3 cups flour, sugar, yeast, and salt in a large mixer bowl.
2. Heat water, milk, and butter until very warm (120° to 130°F).
3. Add liquid ingredients to flour mixture; beat until smooth, about 3 minutes on high speed of electric mixer.
4. Gradually stir in enough more flour to make a soft dough.

5. Turn out onto a floured surface; knead until smooth and elastic (5 to 8 minutes).

6. Shape dough into a ball, place in an oiled bowl, and turn to oil top of dough. Cover; let rise in a warm place until double in bulk (30 to 45 minutes).

7. Punch dough down. Divide in half. Shape each half into rolls (see page 23) for different shapes). Let rise in a warm place until double in bulk (30 to 45 minutes).

8. Bake at 375°F 20 to 25 minutes, or just until rolls begin to change color. Cool in pans 20 minutes. Finish cooling on wire racks. Wrap tightly in plastic bags and refrigerate up to 1 week, or freeze up to 2 months. Before serving, place rolls on ungreased baking sheet.

9. Bake at 400°F 10 to 12 minutes.

Cottage Cheese Rolls

12 ROLLS

¼ cup warm orange juice (105° to 115°F)
1 package active dry yeast
1 cup (8 ounces) creamed cottage cheese
2 teaspoons caraway seed
1 tablespoon sugar
1 teaspoon grated orange peel
1 tablespoon grated onion
1 teaspoon salt
¼ teaspoon baking soda
1 egg, slightly beaten
2⅓ cups sifted all-purpose flour

1. Put orange juice into a warm large bowl. Sprinkle yeast over orange juice and stir until dissolved.

2. Heat cottage cheese in a small saucepan just until lukewarm. Stir cheese into yeast mixture. Add remaining ingredients except flour; mix well. Beat in flour gradually until completely blended, scraping down sides of bowl as necessary; beat vigorously about 20 strokes (dough will be sticky and heavy).

3. Cover bowl with a clean towel; let rise in a warm place about 1 hour, or until double in bulk.

4. Stir dough down. Divide evenly among 12 greased 2½-inch muffin pan wells. Cover with towel; let rise again 35 minutes, or until double in bulk.

5. Bake at 350°F 25 minutes, or until rolls are golden brown and sound hollow when tapped.

6. Remove from pans and serve while hot.

Cottage Cheese Rolls

Better Batter Rolls

2 DOZEN ROLLS

3 cups all-purpose flour
1 package active dry yeast
1 teaspoon salt
1 cup hot water
¼ cup vegetable oil
¼ cup honey
1 egg

1. Combine 2 cups flour, yeast, and salt in a mixer bowl. Add water, oil, honey, and egg; beat until smooth, about 2 minutes on medium speed of electric mixer or 300 vigorous strokes by hand.
2. Beat in remaining flour by hand. Cover; let rise until double in bulk (about 30 minutes).
3. Fill greased muffin-pan wells half full. Let rise until double in bulk (about 30 minutes).
4. Bake at 400°F 10 to 12 minutes.

Brooklyn Bagels

1 DOZEN BAGELS

4 to 5 cups all-purpose flour
1 package active dry yeast
2 teaspoons salt
1½ cups hot water (120° to 130°F)
2 tablespoons honey or sugar
1 egg white
1 teaspoon water

1. Combine 1 cup flour, yeast, and salt in a bowl.
2. Stir in hot water and honey; beat until smooth, about 3 minutes. Stir in enough remaining flour to make a soft dough.
3. Turn out onto a floured surface; continue to work in flour until dough is stiff enough to knead. Knead until smooth and elastic (about 5 minutes).
4. Cover with bowl. Let rest 15 minutes.
5. Divide into 12 equal parts. Shape each into a flattened ball. With thumb and forefinger poke a hole into center. Stretch and rotate until hole enlarges to about 1 or 2 inches. Cover; let rise about 20 minutes.
6. Boil water in a large shallow pan, about 2 inches deep. Reduce heat. Simmer a few bagels at a time about 7 minutes. Remove from pan; drain on a towel about 5 minutes. Place on a baking sheet; brush with mixture of egg white and water.
7. Bake at 375°F 30 minutes, or until done.
8. To serve, split and toast. Spread with **butter** and **jam** or **cream cheese.**

English Muffins

ABOUT 1 DOZEN MUFFINS

3 to 3½ cups all-purpose flour
2 tablespoons sugar
1 package active dry yeast
1 teaspoon salt
¾ cup hot milk (120° to 130°F)
1 egg (at room temperature)
2 tablespoons vegetable oil
Cornmeal

1. Combine 1 cup flour, sugar, yeast, and salt in a mixer bowl.
2. Stir in milk, egg, and oil; beat until smooth, about 3 minutes on high speed of electric mixer.
3. Stir in enough remaining flour to make a soft dough.
4. Turn out onto floured board; knead until smooth and elastic (5 to 8 minutes).
5. Cover with bowl; let rest 20 minutes.
6. Roll out to ½-inch thickness. Cut into 3- or 4-inch rounds. Sprinkle with cornmeal. Cover; let rise until double in bulk (about 45 minutes).
7. Bake in a greased heavy skillet or on a griddle on top of the range over low heat 20 to 30 minutes, or until golden brown, turning once. Cool and store in an airtight container or plastic bag.
8. To serve, split with knife or fork. Toast. Serve hot.

Bagels and English Muffins

Sweet Rolls

16 LARGE
ROLLS

2 packages active dry yeast
½ cup warm water
½ cup sugar
½ teaspoon salt
1 tablespoon anise seed
½ cup butter or margarine,
 melted
3 eggs, at room temperature
3¾ to 4¾ cups all-purpose
 flour
1 egg yolk
2 tablespoons light corn
 syrup

1. Sprinkle yeast over water in a large warm bowl. Stir until yeast is dissolved. Add sugar, salt, anise seed, melted butter, eggs, and 2 cups of flour; beat until smooth. Stir in enough additional flour to make a soft dough.
2. Turn dough onto a lightly floured surface; knead until smooth and elastic (8 to 10 minutes).
3. Put dough into a greased bowl; turn to grease top. Cover; let rise in a warm place until double in bulk (about 1 hour).
4. Punch dough down and turn onto lightly floured surface; roll into a 12-inch square. Cut into fourths and cut each square into 4 triangles.
5. Allowing space for rising, place triangles on greased cookie sheets. Cover; let rise in warm place until double in bulk (about 1 hour).
6. Beat egg yolk and corn syrup together until blended. Generously brush over triangles.
7. Bake at 350°F 10 to 15 minutes. Serve warm.

Crispy Breadsticks

32 BREAD
STICKS

1 cup whole wheat flour
1 package active dry yeast
1 tablespoon sugar
1 teaspoon salt
⅔ cup hot water
2 tablespoons vegetable oil
1 to 1¼ cups all-purpose
 flour

1. Stir together whole wheat flour, yeast, sugar, and salt in a mixing bowl.
2. Blend in water and oil; beat until smooth.
3. Stir in enough flour to form a soft dough.
4. Turn onto a floured surface; continue to work in flour until dough is stiff enough to knead. Knead until smooth and elastic (about 5 minutes), working in as much flour as possible. (The more flour, the crispier the bread sticks.)
5. Cover with bowl; let rest about 30 minutes.
6. Divide dough in quarters. Divide each quarter into 8 equal pieces. For ease in shaping, allow dough to rest about 10 minutes. Roll each piece with palms of hands into 10-inch lengths.
7. Place on greased baking sheets about ½ inch apart. If desired, brush with a mixture of 1 egg white and 1 teaspoon water.
8. Bake at 325°F 20 minutes, or until golden brown and crispy.

Parmesan Bread Finger

32 BREAD
FINGERS

2½ cups all-purpose biscuit
 mix
1 package active dry yeast
½ teaspoon salt
⅔ cup hot water
¼ cup butter or margarine,
 melted
¼ cup grated Parmesan
 cheese

1. Combine biscuit mix, yeast, and salt in a bowl.
2. Stir in water until mixture clings to itself.
3. Turn dough onto a floured surface. Knead 8 to 10 times.
4. Roll out into a 13x9-inch rectangle.
5. Brush half of butter in a 13x9x2-inch baking pan. Place dough in pan, pressing to fit. Cut crosswise into 16 strips, then lengthwise in half.
6. Brush with remaining butter and sprinkle with cheese. Cover; let rise 15 minutes.
7. Bake at 425°F 15 minutes. Turn off oven; allow sticks to remain in oven 15 minutes.

Brioche (page 28)

FLAT BREADS

Tomato-Cheese Pizza

6 TO 8
SERVINGS

½ package active dry yeast
1 cup plus 2 tablespoons
  warm water
4 cups sifted all-purpose
  flour
1 teaspoon salt
3 cups drained canned
  tomatoes
8 ounces mozzarella cheese,
  thinly sliced
½ cup olive oil
¼ cup grated Parmesan
  cheese
1 teaspoon salt
½ teaspoon pepper
2 teaspoons oregano

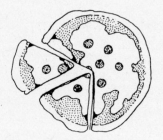

1. Soften yeast in 2 tablespoons warm water. Set aside.
2. Pour remaining cup of warm water into a large bowl. Blend in 2 cups flour and 1 teaspoon salt. Stir softened yeast and add to flour-water mixture, mixing well.
3. Add about 1 cup flour to yeast mixture and beat until very smooth. Mix in enough remaining flour to make a soft dough. Turn dough onto a lightly floured surface and allow to rest 5 to 10 minutes. Knead 5 to 8 minutes, until dough is smooth and elastic.
4. Shape dough into a smooth ball and place in a greased bowl just large enough to allow dough to double. Turn dough to bring greased surface to top. Cover with waxed paper and let stand in warm place (about 80°) until dough is doubled (about 1½ to 2 hours).
5. Punch down with fist. Fold edge towards center and turn dough over. Divide dough into two equal balls. Grease another bowl and place one of the balls in it. Turn dough in both bowls so greased side is on top. Cover and let rise again until almost doubled (about 45 minutes).
6. Roll each ball of dough into a 14x10-inch rectangle, ⅛ inch thick. Place on two lightly greased 15½x12-inch baking sheets. Shape edges by pressing dough between thumb and forefinger to make a ridge. If desired, dough may be rolled into rounds, ⅛ inch thick.
7. Force tomatoes through a sieve or food mill and spread 1½ cups on each pizza. Arrange 4 ounces of mozzarella cheese on each pizza. Sprinkle over each pizza, in the order given, ¼ cup olive oil, 2 tablespoons grated Parmesan cheese, ½ teaspoon salt, ¼ teaspoon pepper, and 1 teaspoon oregano.
8. Bake at 400°F 25 to 30 minutes, or until crust is browned. Cut into wedges to serve.

Mushroom Pizza: Follow Tomato-Cheese Pizza recipe. Before baking, place on each pizza 1 cup (8-ounce can) drained **mushroom buttons.**

Sausage Pizza: Follow Tomato-Cheese Pizza recipe. Before baking, place on each pizza 1 pound **hot Italian sausage** (with casing removed), cut in ¼-inch pieces.

Anchovy Pizza: Follow Tomato-Cheese Pizza recipe. Omit mozzarella and Parmesan cheeses, decrease amount of oregano to ¼ teaspoon, and top each pizza with **anchovy fillets,** cut in ¼-inch pieces.

Miniature Pizzas: Follow Tomato-Cheese Pizza recipe. After rolling dough, cut dough into 3½-inch rounds. Shape edge of rounds as in Tomato-Cheese Pizza recipe. Using half the amount of ingredients in that recipe, spread each pizza with 2 tablespoons sieved canned tomatoes. Top with

(continued)

Tomato-Cheese Pizza

a slice of mozzarella cheese. Sprinkle cheese with ½ teaspoon olive oil, ½ teaspoon grated Parmesan cheese, and a few grains salt and pepper. Bake at 400°F 15 to 20 minutes, or until crust is browned.
ABOUT 24 MINIATURE PIZZAS

English Muffin Pizzas: Split 12 **English muffins** and spread cut sides with **butter or margarine.** Toast under the broiler until lightly browned. Top each half as for Miniature Pizza. Bake at 400°F 5 to 8 minutes, or until tomato mixture is bubbling hot.
24 PIZZAS

Indian Flat Bread

16 ROUND
LOAVES

1 cup all-purpose flour
1 package active dry yeast
2 teaspoons salt
1 cup hot water (120°-130°F)
¼ cup buttermilk or yogurt
1 egg (at room temperature)
2 tablespoons vegetable oil
1 tablespoon honey or sugar
2 to 3 cups all-purpose flour
Melted butter (optional)
Cornmeal or sesame or poppy seeds (optional)

1. Combine 1 cup flour, yeast, and salt in a mixing bowl.
2. Stir in water, buttermilk, egg, oil, and honey; beat until smooth.
3. Stir in enough remaining flour to form a soft, sticky dough.
4. Turn onto a floured surface; continue to work in flour until dough is stiff enough to knead. Knead until smooth and elastic, but still soft (3 to 5 minutes).
5. Place in an oiled bowl, turning once to oil top of dough. Cover; let rise until double in bulk (about 45 minutes).
6. Punch dough down. Shape into 16 equal balls. Let rest 5 minutes. Roll out each ball to a ¼-inch-thick round. If desired, brush with melted butter and sprinkle with cornmeal, sesame, or poppy seeds. Set on baking sheets.
7. Bake at 450°F 5 to 8 minutes.

Pocket Bread

20 POCKET
BREADS

2 cups all-purpose flour
2 packages active dry yeast
2 tablespoons sugar or honey
2 teaspoons salt
2½ cups hot water (120°-130°F)
¼ cup vegetable oil
5½ to 6 cups all-purpose flour

1. Combine 2 cups flour, yeast, sugar, and salt in a large mixing bowl.
2. Stir in water and oil; beat until smooth.
3. Stir in enough remaining flour to make a soft dough.
4. Turn onto a floured surface; continue to work in flour until stiff enough to knead. Knead until smooth and elastic (about 5 minutes).
5. Place in an oiled bowl; turn to oil top of dough. Cover; let rise in a warm place until double in bulk (about 45 minutes).
6. Punch dough down. Divide in half. Divide each half into 10 equal pieces. Roll each piece into a ball. Let dough rest 5 minutes. Roll balls into 3- or 4-inch rounds, ⅛ inch thick. Place on greased baking sheets. Cover; let rise 30 minutes (see Note).
7. Bake at 450°F 5 to 8 minutes, or until puffed and brown.

Note: Avoid punching or creasing dough after rolling, or bread will not puff properly.

SWEET DOUGH

Basic Sweet Dough

4 to 5 cups all-purpose flour
2 packages active dry yeast
1 teaspoon salt
¾ cup milk
½ cup water
½ cup melted butter
½ cup sugar
1 egg

1. Stir together 1¾ cups flour, yeast, and salt in a large mixer bowl.
2. Heat milk, water, butter, and sugar until very warm (120° to 130°F).
3. Add liquid ingredients to flour mixture; beat until smooth, about 2 minutes on electric mixer.
4. Add egg and ½ cup more flour and beat another 2 minutes.
5. Gradually add enough more flour to make a soft dough.
6. Turn out onto floured board; continue to work in flour until dough can be kneaded. Knead until smooth and elastic, but still soft (about 5 minutes).
7. Cover; let rest about 20 minutes.
8. Shape, let rise, and bake as directed in recipes that follow.

Cinnamon Rolls: Roll dough into a 13x9-inch rectangle. Spread with **2 tablespoons softened butter** or **margarine.** Sprinkle with mixture of **½ cup firmly packed brown** or **white sugar** and **2 teaspoons cinnamon.** Beginning with long side, roll dough up tightly jelly-roll fashion. Cut roll into 12 (1-inch) slices. Place slices in a greased 13x9x2-inch baking pan or greased muffin cups. Bake at 375°F 15 to 20 minutes.
1½ DOZEN

Glazed Raised Doughnuts: Follow recipe for Basic Sweet Dough. Roll out to about ½-inch thickness. Cut with doughnut cutter or make into shape of your choice, such as squares, twists, long johns, doughnut holes, or bismarcks. Let rise, uncovered, until light, 40 to 50 minutes. Fry in deep hot oil (375°F) 3 to 4 minutes, turning once. Drain on paper towels. Dip in a glaze of **1½ cups confectioners' sugar, 2 tablespoons warm water,** and **1 teaspoon vanilla extract.**

Apricot Crisscross Coffeecake: For one large coffeecake, roll dough into a 15x12-inch rectangle. For two small coffeecakes, divide dough in half. Roll each half into a 12x8-inch rectangle. Combine **½ cup apricot preserves, ½ cup raisins,** and **½ cup sliced almonds.** Spread half the filling lengthwise down the center of each rectangle. Make about 12 slashes, each 2 inches long, down the long sides of each coffeecake. Fold strips alternately over filling, herringbone fashion. Cover; let rise until double in bulk (50 to 60 minutes). Bake at 375°F 20 to 25 minutes for small coffeecakes and 35 to 40 minutes for large coffeecake.

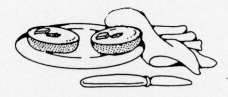

Refrigerator Sweet Dough

2 COFFEECAKES

5 to 6 cups all-purpose flour
2 packages active dry yeast
½ cup sugar
1½ teaspoons salt
1 cup milk
½ cup water
½ cup butter or margarine,
softened
2 eggs

1. Stir 1¾ cups flour, yeast, sugar, and salt together in a large mixer bowl.
2. Heat milk, water, and butter to very warm (120° to 130°F).
3. Add liquid to dry ingredients and beat until smooth, about 2 minutes on electric mixer.
4. Add eggs and ½ cup flour and continue beating another 2 minutes.
5. Gradually stir in enough additional flour to make a soft dough.
6. Turn out onto floured board; continue to work in flour until dough can be kneaded. Knead until smooth and elastic, but still soft (5 to 8 minutes).
7. Cover with plastic wrap, then with a towel.
8. Let rest 20 minutes.
9. Divide in half and shape as desired.
10. Brush with oil. Cover with plastic wrap.
11. Refrigerate 2 to 24 hours. When ready to bake, remove from refrigerator and let stand 10 minutes.
12. Bake at 375°F 20 to 30 minutes.
13. Remove from pans and cool on rack.

Cinnamon Slice Coffeecake: Follow shaping instructions as in Cinnamon Rolls (page 39), only omit 13x9x2-inch pan. Instead, place 6 slices, cut-side down, on bottom of a greased 10-inch tube pan. Place 6 more slices cut-side against outer side of pan. Cover first layer with remaining 6 rolls. Bake at 375°F 20 to 25 minutes.

Cinnamon Discs: Combine **¾ cup firmly packed brown sugar, ¾ cup white sugar, ½ cup finely chopped pecans,** and **1 teaspoon cinnamon.** Divide dough in half. Roll each half into a 12-inch square. Melt **½ cup butter.** Brush dough with 2 tablespoons of the butter. Sprinkle with ⅓ cup sugar mixture. Roll up jelly-roll fashion; pinch to seal edges. Cut into 1-inch slices. Place on greased baking sheets at least 3 inches apart. Cover with waxed paper. Flatten each to about 3 inches in diameter. Let rise 15 minutes. Flatten again. Brush with remaining butter; sprinkle with remaining sugar mixture. Cover with waxed paper; flatten again. Bake at 400°F 10 to 12 minutes.
2 DOZEN

Bubble Bread: Divide dough into 20 equal pieces; shape into balls. Combine **½ cup sugar or firmly packed brown sugar, ½ cup finely chopped nuts,** and **1 teaspoon cinnamon.** Melt **½ cup butter or margarine.** Roll balls in butter, then in sugar mixture. Arrange balls in a well-greased 10-inch tube pan. Cover; let rise until double in bulk (45 to 60 minutes). Bake at 350°F 30 to 35 minutes.

Orange Bubble Ring: Shape dough into 20 balls as for Bubble Bread. Roll each ball in **½ cup melted butter** and then a mixture of **½ cup sugar** and **1 tablespoon grated orange peel.** Arrange and bake as above.

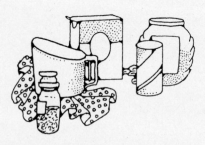

Greek Easter Bread

1 LARGE LOAF

2 packages active dry yeast
½ cup warm water
½ cup milk, scalded and cooled
1 cup unsalted butter, melted and cooled to lukewarm
4 eggs, slightly beaten
1 egg yolk
¾ cup sugar
1 tablespoon anise seed, crushed
1 teaspoon salt
7 cups all-purpose flour
1 egg white, slightly beaten
¼ cup sesame seed

1. Blend yeast with warm water in a large bowl and stir until dissolved. Add milk, butter, eggs, egg yolk, sugar, anise seed, and salt; blend thoroughly. Add flour gradually, beating until smooth.
2. Turn dough onto a lightly floured board and knead for 10 minutes, or until dough is smooth and elastic.
3. Place dough in a lightly oiled large bowl, turning dough to coat surface. Cover and let rise in a warm place for about 2 hours, or until double in bulk. Test by inserting a finger about ½ inch in dough. If indentation remains, the dough is ready to shape.
4. Punch dough down. Knead on unfloured board to make a smooth ball. Cut off four pieces, each the size of a large egg. Place remaining dough in a greased round pan, 10 inches in diameter and 2 inches high. Shape small pieces into twists about 4½ inches long. Arrange the twists from the center of the dough so they radiate out to the edge. Brush the loaf lightly with beaten egg white. Sprinkle with sesame seed. Cover loaf lightly and set in a warm place until double in bulk (about 1½ hours).
5. Bake at 375°F for 30 minutes, or until a wooden pick inserted in center of loaf comes out clean. Transfer to wire rack to cool.

Note: For Easter, place a red egg in center of the dough in pan. Shape small pieces of dough into loops and place a red egg in the center of each.

New Year's Day Bread: Follow recipe for Greek Easter Bread; substitute **grated peel of 1 large orange** for the anise seed. Wrap a coin in foil and knead into the dough. Proceed as directed.

Easter Egg Bread

1 LARGE
WREATH

2 packages active dry yeast
½ cup warm water
1 cup all-purpose flour
⅓ cup water
¾ cup butter or margarine
1 tablespoon grated lemon
  peel
1½ tablespoons lemon juice
¾ cup sugar
1 teaspoon salt
2 eggs, well beaten
3¾ to 4¼ cups all-purpose
  flour
6 colored eggs (uncooked)

1. Soften yeast in the warm water in a bowl. Mix in the 1 cup flour, then the ⅓ cup water. Beat until smooth. Cover; let rise in a warm place until doubled (about 1 hour).
2. Cream butter with lemon peel and juice. Add beaten eggs in halves, beating thoroughly after each addition.
3. Add yeast mixture and beat until blended. Add about half of the remaining flour and beat thoroughly. Beat in enough flour to make a soft dough.
4. Knead on floured surface until smooth. Put into a greased deep bowl; turn dough to bring greased surface to top. Cover; let rise in a warm place until doubled.
5. Punch down dough; divide into thirds. Cover; let rest about 10 minutes.
6. With hands, roll and stretch each piece into a roll about 26 inches long and ¾ inch thick. Loosely braid rolls together. On a lightly greased baking sheet or jelly-roll pan shape into a ring, pressing ends together. At even intervals, gently spread dough apart and tuck in a colored egg. Cover; let rise again until doubled.
7. Bake at 375°F about 30 minutes. During baking check bread for browning, and when sufficiently browned, cover loosely with aluminum foil.
8. Transfer coffee cake to a wire rack. If desired, spread a confectioners' sugar icing over top of warm bread.

Greek Christmas Bread

2 LOAVES

2 envelopes active dry yeast
2 cups scalded milk, cooled
  to 105° to 115°F
1 cup sugar
1 teaspoon salt
4 eggs (or 8 yolks), well
  beaten
½ cup unsalted butter,
  melted
7½ to 8 cups all-purpose
  flour
1½ teaspoons cardamom,
  pounded, or 1 teaspoon
  mastic
½ cup dried golden currants
¾ cup chopped walnuts
2 egg whites, beaten
3 to 4 tablespoons sugar

1. Sprinkle yeast over 1 cup warm milk in a small bowl; stir until dissolved. Set aside.
2. Reserve 2 teaspoons sugar for pounding with mastic, if using. Put sugar into a bowl and add salt, eggs, remaining 1 cup milk, and butter; mix well.
3. Put 7 cups flour into a large bowl. Stir in cardamom, or pound mastic with 2 teaspoons sugar (so it will not become gummy) and add. Make a well and add dissolved yeast, egg mixture, currants, and nuts; mix well.
4. Knead dough on a floured board, adding the remaining 1 cup flour as required. Knead dough until smooth (5 to 6 minutes).
5. Place dough in a greased bowl. Turn until surface is completely greased. Cover. Set in a warm place until double in bulk.
6. Punch dough down. Form into two round loaves and place in buttered 10-inch pans.
7. Cover and let rise again in a warm place until double in bulk.
8. Bake at 375°F 15 minutes. Remove from oven and brush with beaten egg whites, then sprinkle with sugar. Return to oven. Turn oven control to 325°F and bake about 35 to 40 minutes, or until bread is done.

Island Bread

Island Bread

1 LOAF

2 packages active dry yeast
1½ cups warm water (105°
   to 115°F)
¼ cup packed dark brown
   sugar
2 tablespoons honey
3 cups whole wheat flour
¼ cup olive oil
2 tablespoons grated orange
   peel
1 tablespoon grated lemon
   peel
2½ teaspoons salt
1 teaspoon anise seed,
   crushed
2 cups all-purpose flour

1. Dissolve yeast in warm water; stir in brown sugar, honey, and whole wheat flour. Beat with a wooden spoon until smooth. Cover and let rise in a warm place until almost double in bulk (about 2 hours).

2. Stir in oil, orange and lemon peels, salt, and anise seed. Gradually add 1¾ cups all-purpose flour, beating vigorously. Cover for 10 minutes.

3. Sprinkle remaining ¼ cup flour on a board and work it in. Put dough on board, cover, and let rise until double in bulk. Shape into a round loaf; put onto a well-greased cookie sheet.

4. Let rise until dough is double in bulk.

5. Bake at 375°F 45 minutes. Turn out of pan immediately and cool on a rack.

Fruit Bread, Milan Style

Fruit Bread, Milan Style

2 LOAVES

2 packages active dry yeast
¼ cup warm water
1 cup butter, melted
1 cup sugar
1 teaspoon salt
2 cups sifted all-purpose
  flour
½ cup milk, scalded and
  cooled to lukewarm
2 eggs
4 egg yolks
3½ cups all-purpose flour
1 cup dark seedless raisins
¾ cup chopped citron
½ cup all-purpose flour
1 egg, slightly beaten
1 tablespoon water

1. Dissolve yeast in the warm water.
2. Pour melted butter into large bowl of electric mixer. Add the sugar and salt gradually, beating constantly.
3. Beating thoroughly after each addition, alternately add the 2 cups flour in thirds and lukewarm milk in halves to the butter mixture. Add yeast and beat well.
4. Combine eggs and egg yolks and beat until thick and piled softly. Add the beaten eggs all at one time to yeast mixture and beat well. Beating thoroughly after each addition, gradually add the 3½ cups flour. Stir in raisins and citron.
5. Sift half of the remaining ½ cup flour over a pastry canvas or board. Turn dough onto floured surface; cover and let rest 10 minutes.
6. Sift remaining flour over dough. Pull dough from edges toward center until flour is worked in. (It will be sticky.) Put dough into a greased deep bowl and grease top of dough. Cover; let rise in a warm place (about 80°F) about 2½ hours.
7. Punch down dough and pull edges of dough in to center. Let rise again about 1 hour.
8. Divide dough into halves and shape each into a round loaf. Put each loaf into a well-greased 8-inch layer cake pan. Brush surfaces generously with a mixture of slightly beaten egg and water. Cover; let rise again about 1 hour.
9. Bake at 350°F 40 to 45 minutes, or until golden brown. Remove to wire racks to cool.

Raised Cornmeal Muffins

1½ TO
2 DOZEN
MUFFINS

5 to 5¼ cups sifted enriched
  all-purpose flour
½ cup sugar
1 tablespoon salt
2 packages active dry yeast
2¼ cups milk
½ cup shortening
2 eggs
1 cup enriched yellow
  cornmeal
Butter or margarine, melted

1. Mix 2¾ cups flour, sugar, salt, and undissolved yeast thoroughly in a large mixer bowl.
2. Put milk and shortening into a saucepan. Set over low heat until very warm (120-130°). Add liquid mixture gradually to dry ingredients while mixing until blended. Beat 2 minutes at medium speed of electric mixer, scraping bowl occasionally. Mix in eggs and 1¾ cups flour, or enough to make a batter. Beat at high speed 2 minutes, scraping bowl occasionally. Blend in cornmeal and enough of the remaining flour to make a smooth, thick batter.
3. Cover; let rise in a warm place until double in bulk (1 to 1½ hours).
4. Beat batter down. Cut against side of bowl with a large spoon enough batter at one time to fill each greased 2½- or 3-inch muffin-pan well two-thirds full, pushing batter with a rubber spatula directly into well. Cover; let rise again until almost double in bulk (about 30 minutes).
5. Bake at 400°F about 20 minutes. Brush tops with melted butter. Remove from pan and serve piping hot.

Note: If desired, mix 1 teaspoon crushed herb, such as chervil, oregano, rosemary, or thyme with flour before adding to batter.

Kugelhupf

2 LARGE OR
3 SMALL
LOAVES

3 to 4 cups all-purpose flour
2 packages active dry yeast
1 cup milk
1 cup raisins
½ cup water
½ cup sugar
½ cup butter
1 teaspoon salt
3 eggs (at room temperature)
2 teaspoons rum extract
Butter, softened
⅓ cup ground almonds
Sifted confectioners' sugar
Candied fruits and nuts
Corn syrup

1. Combine 2 cups flour and yeast in a large mixer bowl.
2. Heat milk, raisins, water, sugar, ½ cup butter, and salt in a saucepan over low heat until very warm (120° to 130°F), stirring to blend; add to flour-yeast mixture and beat until smooth, about 3 minutes on medium speed of electric mixer. Blend in eggs and rum extract; add ½ cup flour and continue to beat 2 minutes. Add enough flour to make a thick batter. Cover; let rise in a warm place until double in bulk and batter is bubbly (about 1 hour).
3. Stir batter down. Spoon into two 1½-quart or three 1-quart turk's-head or other fancy molds that have been buttered and dusted with ground almonds. Cover; let rise in a warm place until double in bulk (about 30 minutes).
4. Bake at 325°F 1 hour for 1½-quart loaves or 45 minutes for 1-quart loaves. If necessary to prevent excessing browning, cover during the last 10 minutes of baking. Unmold on wire racks. Dust with confectioners' sugar. Decorate with candied fruits and nuts that have been dipped in corn syrup.

Austrian Almond Bread

2 LARGE
LOAVES

5 to 5½ cups all-purpose
flour
2 packages active dry yeast
1 cup milk
½ cup sugar
½ cup shortening or butter
¼ cup butter
2 teaspoons salt
2 eggs (at room temperature)
½ cup golden raisins
½ cup candied mixed fruit,
chopped
½ cup chopped blanched
almonds
Almond Icing (below)
Candied fruit and nuts for
decoration (optional)

1. Combine 2 cups flour and yeast in a large mixer bowl.
2. Heat milk, sugar, shortening, water, and salt in a saucepan over low heat until very warm (120° to 130°F), stirring to blend. Add liquid to flour-yeast mixture and beat until smooth, about 3 minutes on medium speed of electric mixer. Blend in eggs. Add 1 cup flour and beat 1 minute. Stir in fruit and almonds; add more flour to make a soft dough.
3. Turn dough onto a lightly floured surface; knead until smooth and satiny (5 to 10 minutes). Cover dough and let rest 20 minutes. Divide dough in half.
4. For each braid, take two-thirds of one portion of dough and divide into thirds. Roll each piece with hands into a 15-inch strand. Braid strands on lightly greased baking sheet. Divide remaining third into thirds; form three 18-inch

strands. Braid strands loosely; place on first braid, pressing in lightly. Tuck ends of top braid under ends of bottom braid. Brush with oil. Let rise in a warm place until double in bulk (about 45 minutes).

5. Bake at 350°F 25 to 30 minutes, or until golden brown. Remove from baking sheets to wire rack. While braids are still slightly warm, ice with almond icing. Decorate with candied fruit and nuts, if desired.

Almond Icing: Put **1½ cups confectioners' sugar, 2 tablespoons milk,** and **1 teaspoon almond extract** into a small bowl; stir until smooth.

Date Nut Bread

Date Nut Bread

3 LOAVES
BREAD

½ cup warm water
2 packages active dry yeast
1¾ cups warm milk
2 tablespoons sugar
1 tablespoon salt
3 tablespoons margarine
5 to 5½ cups sifted enriched
   all-purpose flour
1 cup whole wheat flour
1 cup chopped dates
½ cup chopped pecans
1 teaspoon ground cinnamon
Peanut Oil
Margarine (optional)

1. Measure warm water into a warm large bowl. Sprinkle in yeast; stir until dissolved. Add warm milk, sugar, salt, and margarine. Stir in 2 cups all-purpose flour. Beat with rotary beater until smooth (about 1 minute). Add 1 cup all-purpose flour; beat with rotary beater until smooth (about 1 minute). Add 1 cup all-purpose flour; beat vigorously with a wooden spoon until smooth (about 150 strokes). Stir in whole wheat flour, dates, pecans, cinnamon, and enough of the remaining all-purpose flour to make a soft dough.

2. Turn dough onto a lightly floured surface. Knead 8 to 10 minutes, or until dough is smooth, elastic, and shows small blisters under surface when drawn tight. Cover with plastic wrap, then a towel. Let rest 20 minutes.

3. Punch dough down. Divide into 3 equal portions. Roll

(continued)

each into a 12x7-inch rectangle. Shape into loaves. Place in 3 greased 7x4x2-inch loaf pans. Brush loaves with oil. Cover pans loosely with plastic wrap. Refrigerate 2 to 24 hours.

4. When ready to bake, remove loaves from refrigerator. Uncover dough carefully. Let stand uncovered 10 minutes at room temperature. Puncture with a greased wooden pick or metal skewer any gas bubbles which may have formed.

5. Bake at 400°F about 35 minutes. Remove from pans immediately, place on wire racks to cool, and, if desired, brush with margarine.

Sweet Maple Coffeecake

2 LOAVES

3 to 3½ cups all-purpose flour
1 package active dry yeast
½ teaspoon salt
½ cup milk
¼ cup water
¼ cup butter or margarine
2 eggs
¼ cup honey or sugar
Maple Filling

1. Combine 1 cup flour, yeast, and salt in a mixer bowl.
2. Warm milk, water, and butter in a small saucepan.
3. Add liquid, eggs, and honey to flour mixture; beat until smooth, about 3 minutes on electric mixer.
4. Stir in enough remaining flour to make a soft, sticky dough.
5. Turn out onto floured board; continue to work in flour until dough can be kneaded. Knead until smooth and elastic, but still soft (about 5 minutes).
6. Cover with a bowl; let rest 30 minutes.
7. Divide dough in half; roll each half into a 15x12-inch rectangle. Spread with Maple Filling. Fold each rectangle in thirds, making a 15x4-inch strip. Cut in 10 equal pieces. Place strips of dough in greased 8x4x2-inch loaf pans, cut side down. Cover; let rise 30 minutes.
8. Bake at 350°F 35 to 40 minutes.

Maple Filling: Cream ½ cup firmly packed brown sugar and ⅓ cup white sugar with ¼ cup softened butter or margarine. Stir in ¼ cup maple syrup, 2 tablespoons all-purpose flour, ½ teaspoon cinnamon, and ½ cup chopped nuts.

Sally Lunn

ONE LARGE LOAF

5 cups all-purpose flour
½ cup sugar
1 package active dry yeast
1 teaspoon salt
1½ cups milk
½ cup butter or margarine
3 eggs
¼ cup sugar
¼ teaspoon nutmeg

1. Combine 2 cups flour, ½ cup sugar, yeast, and salt in a mixer bowl.
2. Heat milk and butter in a small saucepan.
3. Add liquid with eggs to flour mixture; beat 2 minutes by hand or with electric mixer.
4. Stir in remaining flour by hand. Cover; let rise until double in bulk (about 1 hour).
5. Stir dough down. Pour into a greased and sugared 10-inch tube pan. Cover; let rise until double in bulk (about 30 minutes).
6. Combine ¼ cup sugar and nutmeg; sprinkle over dough.
7. Bake at 400°F 40 minutes. Cool in pan 5 minutes.
8. If desired, serve hot with strawberries and whipped cream.

Russian Kulich

2 LARGE
OR 3 MEDIUM
LOAVES

5 cups all-purpose flour
2 packages active dry yeast
1 cup milk
½ cup sugar
¼ cup oil
2 teaspoons salt
2 eggs (at room temperature)
2 teaspoons grated lemon
  peel
½ cup chopped blanched
  almonds
¼ cup raisins
¼ cup chopped candied
  citron
¼ cup chopped candied
  orange peel
¼ cup chopped candied
  cherries
½ cup confectioners' sugar
1 tablespoon milk
Candied fruit (optional)

1. Combine 1 cup flour and yeast in a large mixer bowl.
2. Heat 1 cup milk, sugar, oil, and salt in a saucepan over low heat until very warm (120° to 130°F), stirring to blend. Add liquid to flour-yeast mixture and beat until smooth, about 2 minutes on medium speed of electric mixer. Beat in eggs, lemon peel, almonds, raisins, and candied fruit. Add 1 cup flour and beat 1 minute on medium speed. Stir in more flour to make a soft dough.
3. Turn dough onto a lightly floured surface and knead until smooth and satiny (8 to 10 minutes). Shape into a ball and place in a lightly greased bowl; turn to grease surface. Cover; let rise in a warm place until double in bulk (about 1½ hours).
4. Punch dough down; divide into 2 or 3 equal portions and shape into balls. Let rest 10 minutes.
5. Grease generously two 46-ounce juice cans or three 1-pound coffee cans. Place dough in cans, filling about half full; brush with oil. Let rise until double in bulk (about 1 hour).
6. Bake at 350°F 30 to 35 minutes, or until golden brown. Immediately remove from cans and cool.
7. Blend confectioners' sugar and 1 tablespoon milk until smooth; ice top of loaves. Decorate with candied fruit, if desired.

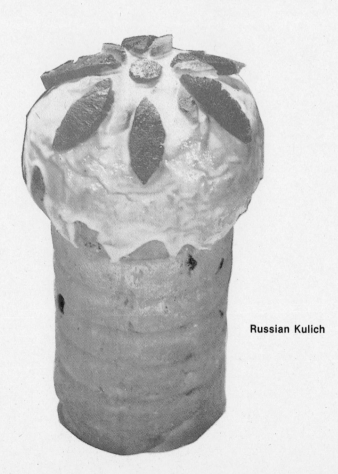

Russian Kulich

Nutty Sweet Twists

2 DOZEN LONG
(6-INCH) TWISTS
OR 4 DOZEN
SHORT (3-INCH)
TWISTS

1 can (13 ounces) evaporated
milk or 1⅔ cups milk
1 tablespoon lemon juice or
vinegar
½ cup raisins
3 tablespoons sugar
2 tablespoons butter or
margarine
3 to 3¼ cups all-purpose
flour
1 package active dry yeast
1 teaspoon salt
½ teaspoon baking soda
1 egg
2 tablespoons butter or
margarine, softened or
melted
⅓ cup firmly packed brown
sugar
⅓ cup finely chopped nuts
2 teaspoons cinnamon

1. Warm milk and lemon juice in a small saucepan. Add raisins, sugar, and 2 tablespoons butter.
2. Combine 2 cups flour, yeast, salt, and baking soda in a large mixer bowl. Stir in milk mixture and egg; beat until smooth.
3. Stir in enough remaining flour to make a soft, sticky dough.
4. Turn out onto a floured surface; continue to work in flour until dough can be kneaded. Knead until smooth and elastic, but still soft (about 5 minutes). Let dough rest 5 minutes.
5. Roll dough into a 24x12-inch rectangle about ⅜ inch thick. Spread or brush with 2 tablespoons butter. Sprinkle with a mixture of brown sugar, nuts, and cinnamon. Fold in half lengthwise, forming a 24x6-inch rectangle. Cut into 1-inch strips. For each roll, hold both ends of strip and twist. Place on greased baking sheet. (If shorter rolls are desired, cut twists in half.)
6. Bake at 375°F 10 to 15 minutes (see Note).

Note: For shinier twists, brush dough with mixture of **1 egg white** and **1 teaspoon water** just before baking.

Frosted Sweet Twists: Follow recipe for Nutty Sweet Twists and glaze baked rolls with a mixture of ½ **cup confectioners' sugar** and **1 tablespoon milk.**

King's Bread Ring

1 LARGE
BREAD RING

2 packages active dry yeast
or 2 cakes compressed
yeast
½ cup warm water (hot for
dry yeast, lukewarm for
compressed)
½ cup milk, scalded
⅓ cup sugar
⅓ cup shortening
2 teaspoons salt
4 cups all-purpose flour
(about)
3 eggs, well beaten
2 cups chopped candied
fruits (citron, cherries, and
orange peel)
Melted butter or margarine
Confectioners' Sugar Icing

1. Soften yeast in water.
2. Pour hot milk over sugar, shortening, and salt in large bowl, stirring until sugar is dissolved and shortening melted. Cool to lukewarm. Beat in 1 cup of the flour, then eggs and softened yeast. Add enough more flour to make a stiff dough. Stir in 1½ cups candied fruits, reserving remainder to decorate baked ring.
3. Turn dough onto a floured surface and knead until smooth and satiny. Roll dough under hands into a long rope; shape into a ring, sealing ends together. Transfer to a greased cookie sheet. Push a tiny china doll into dough so it is completely covered. Brush with melted butter.
4. Coveer with a towel and let rise in a warm place until double in bulk (about 1½ hours).
5. Bake at 375°F 25 to 30 minutes, or until golden brown.
6. Cool on wire rack. Frost with Confectioners' Sugar Icing and decorate with reserved candied fruit.

Confectioners' Sugar Icing: Blend **1⅓ cups confectioners' sugar, 4 teaspoons water,** and **½ teaspoon vanilla extract.**

King's Bread Ring

Cottage Raisin Puffs

2 DOZEN

3 to 3½ cups all-purpose
   flour
2 packages active dry yeast
1½ teaspoons salt
1 cup creamed cottage cheese
½ cup melted butter or
   margarine
½ cup hot water
¼ cup sugar or honey
1 egg
Raisin Cream Filling

1. Combine 1 cup flour, yeast, and salt in a mixer bowl.
2. Heat cottage cheese, butter, water, and sugar in a saucepan until very warm (120° to 130°F).
3. Add liquid and egg to flour mixture and beat until smooth, about 3 minutes.
4. Stir in enough remaining flour to make a soft dough.
5. Turn out onto floured board; continue to work in flour until dough can be kneaded. Knead until smooth and elastic, but still soft (about 5 minutes).
6. Place in an oiled bowl; turn to oil top of dough. Cover; let rise in warm place until double in bulk (about 1 hour).
7. Punch dough down. Roll into a rectangle 20x12 inches. Cut into 2-inch squares. Place about 1 teaspoon of Raisin Cream Filling in center of each square. Bring corners to center and press together. Place on greased baking sheets. Let rise 10 minutes.
8. Bake at 375°F 12 to 15 minutes, or until done.

Raisin Cream Filling: Stir **2 tablespoons milk** into **1 package (8 ounces) cream cheese, softened.** Blend in ½ **cup raisins.**

Cottage Date Puffs: Prepare Cottage Raisin Puffs, substituting **chopped dates** for raisins and adding ¼ **cup chopped nuts.**

SOURDOUGH

Sourdough Starter

2 cups flour
1 package active dry yeast
1 tablespoon sugar
2 cups warm potato water
   (105° to 115°)

1. Combine flour, yeast, and sugar in a nonmetal mixing bowl. Stir in potato water.
2. Cover; let stand in a warm place (80° to 85°F) for 48 hours.
3. Store in covered jar in refrigerator.

To use in recipe: Stir well before use. Pour out required amount called for in recipe and use as directed.

To replenish remaining starter: Mix in 1 cup each flour and warm water until smooth. Let stand in warm place a few hours until it bubbles again before covering and replacing in refrigerator.

Note: Use in recipe or remove 1 cup starter and replenish every week.

Sourdough Sam's Skillet Loaves (page 54)

San Francisco Sourdough French Bread

1 LOAF

1 cup sourdough starter
  (page 52)
1½ cups warm water
2 tablespoons sugar
5 to 6 cups all-purpose flour
1 tablespoon salt
½ teaspoon baking soda

1. Combine starter, water, sugar, and 3 cups flour in a large nonmetal mixing bowl. Cover with plastic wrap or a towel; let stand at room temperature 12 hours or overnight.
2. Combine salt, soda, and 1 cup flour. Stir into dough; beat until smooth.
3. Stir in enough remaining flour to make a soft dough.
4. Turn dough onto a floured surface; continue to work in flour until dough is stiff enough to knead. Knead until smooth and elastic (5 to 8 minutes).
5. Shape dough into a long, narrow loaf by rolling and stretching dough as for French Bread (page #). Place on a greased baking sheet. Cover; let rise in a warm place until double in bulk (1½ to 2 hours).
6. With a sharp knife, slash top ½ inch deep at 2-inch intervals. Brush loaf with **water**.
7. Bake at 375°F 30 to 35 minutes.

Note: For a browner and shinier crust, brush before baking with a mixture of **1 egg white** and ⅓ **cup water** instead of only water.

Sourdough Sam's Skillet Loaves (Pictured on page 53)

2 LOAVES

1 cup sourdough starter
2½ cups warm water
2 tablespoons honey or sugar
7 to 7½ cups all-purpose
  flour
¼ cup vegetable oil
1 tablespoon salt
1 teaspoon baking soda
6 tablespoons butter
4 tablespoons cornmeal

1. Combine starter, water, honey, and 5 cups flour in a large nonmetal mixing bowl. Cover with plastic wrap or a wet towel; let stand at room temperature 12 hours or overnight.
2. Stir in oil. Combine salt, soda, and 1 cup flour. Stir into dough; beat until smooth.
3. Stir in enough remaining flour to make a soft dough.
4. Turn dough onto a floured surface; continue to work in flour until dough is stiff enough to knead. Knead until smooth and elastic (about 5 minutes).
5. Divide dough in half. Roll each into a 10-inch round (see Note).
6. For each loaf, melt 3 tablespoons butter in a heavy 10-inch cast-iron skillet with heat-resistant handle. Sprinkle with 2 tablespoons cornmeal. Place dough in skillet. Turn over to coat top with butter and cornmeal. Let rise 15 minutes.
7. Bake at 400°F 25 to 30 minutes, or until done.
8. Serve hot with **butter** and **honey**.

Note: If you don't have 2 skillets, simply allow the second dough circle to rise while the first bakes – it will just have a lighter texture.

Sweet and Sourdough Granola Bread: Prepare dough as in Sourdough Sam's Skillet Loaves. After dividing dough in half, roll out each half into a 16x6-inch rectangle. Brush each with **2 tablespoons melted butter** and sprinkle with half the Granola Cinnamon Filling. Beginning with narrow end of rectangle, roll up tightly as for jelly roll; seal edges.

Place loaves in 2 greased 9x5x3-inch loaf pans. Cover; let rise until double in bulk (45 to 60 minutes). Bake at 350°F 40 to 45 minutes.

Granola Cinnamon Filling: Combine **1 cup granola, ½ cup firmly packed brown sugar, ½ cup chopped dates or raisins** (optional), and **1 teaspoon cinnamon.**

Sourdough Apple Kuchen: Prepare dough as in Sourdough Sam's Skillet Loaves. After dividing dough, roll out each half into a 10-inch round. Place dough in 2 greased 9- or 10-inch springform pans. Press dough about 1½ inches up sides of pan. Fill each kuchen with a mixture of **2 cups finely sliced pared apples, ½ cup firmly packed brown sugar, ¼ cup all-purpose flour,** and **1 teaspoon cinnamon.** Sprinkle with **¼ cup sliced almonds.** Dot with 2 tablespoons butter. Let rise 30 minutes. Bake at 375°F 40 to 45 minutes, or until done.

Golden Sourdough Bread

2 LOAVES

1 package active dry yeast
1¼ cups warm water
¼ cup firmly packed brown sugar
2 teaspoons salt
⅓ cup butter or margarine
3½ to 4 cups all-purpose flour
1½ cups sourdough starter (page 52)
3½ cups uncooked oats

1. Soften yeast in ¼ cup warm water. Pour remaining 1 cup water over sugar, salt, and butter in a large bowl. Stir in 2 cups of flour, sourdough starter, oats, and softened yeast. Stir in enough additional flour to make a stiff dough.
2. Knead dough on a floured surface until smooth and elastic (about 10 minutes). Round dough into a ball; place in a greased bowl. Lightly grease surface of dough. Cover; let rise in a warm place until nearly double in bulk (about 1 hour).
3. Punch dough down; shape into 2 round loaves. Place on greased cookie sheets. Let rise in a warm place until nearly double in bulk (about 40 minutes). Slash tops with sharp knife or kitchen shears.
4. Bake at 400°F 35 to 40 minutes. Cool on wire racks.

Golden Sourdough Bread

Quick Breads

Quick breads get their names from the relatively short time of preparation as compared with yeast breads. The leavening of quick breads is usually achieved by the use of baking powder or baking soda. Popovers are an exception, requiring steam to leaven them. Quick breads include different types of products—muffins, biscuits, loaves (fruit and nut), popovers, corn bread, dumplings, brown bread, waffles, griddlecakes, some doughnuts and fritters.

One method of classifying quick breads is by the proportion of liquid to flour. **Thin batters** (popovers, timbales, griddlecakes)—usually 1½ to 2 cups liquid to 2 cups flour. **Stiff batters** (muffins, fruit and nut loaves)—usually 1 cup liquid to 2 cups flour. **Soft doughs** (doughnuts, baking powder biscuits)—usually ¾ cup liquid to 2 cups flour.

Quick breads do not have the keeping quality that richer products do because they are low in ingredients such as shortening eggs and sugar.

Most quick breads are at their peak in flavor when served fresh from the oven. Many of the loaves that have higher amounts of sugar and shortening along with fruits and nuts are usually cooled before serving. Some loaves slice more easily and improve in flavor if they are served the following day.

An important reminder—never overmix a quick bread batter or dough.

Quick Applesauce Bread

LOAVES

Quick Applesauce Bread

1 LOAF

2¼ cups Basic Oats Mix
(page 67)
1 cup sugar
1 teaspoon cinnamon
1 cup canned sweetened
applesauce
1 egg
½ cup milk
½ cup raisins

1. Combine Oats Mix, sugar, and cinnamon in a bowl. Add applesauce, egg, milk, and raisins; stir until mixed.
2. Turn batter into a greased and floured 8½x4½x2½-inch loaf pan.
3. Bake at 350°F 55 to 60 minutes.
4. Remove from pan and cool completely on a rack before slicing.

Oklahoma Oatmeal Bread

1 LARGE LOAF
OR 2 SMALL
LOAVES

1 cup evaporated milk
2 tablespoons vegetable oil
1 tablespoon vinegar
1 cup uncooked oats
1 cup all-purpose flour
1 cup firmly packed brown
sugar
1 teaspoon baking soda
½ teaspoon salt
1 cup raisins or chopped
nuts

1. Beat milk, oil, and vinegar in a mixing bowl until smooth.
2. Add oats, flour, brown sugar, baking soda, and salt; mix until well blended.
3. Stir in raisins or nuts.
4. Turn into a greased 9x5x3-inch loaf pan or two 7x4x2-inch loaf pans.
5. Bake at 350°F 50 to 60 minutes, or until done.
6. Cool before wrapping.

Orange Soda Bread

1 LOAF

3½ cups all-purpose flour
1 teaspoon salt
1 teaspoon sugar
1 teaspoon baking powder
1 cup buttermilk
½ cup fresh orange juice
1 egg
1 cup raisins
1 tablespoon grated orange
peel

1. Combine flour, salt, sugar, and baking soda in a bowl. Make a well in the center and pour in buttermilk and orange juice; mix well.
2. Add egg, raisin, and orange peel; beat until smooth (dough will be sticky).
3. Knead lightly on a well-floured surface. Shape into a round loaf and put into a well-greased 9-inch round layer cake pan. Cut an X across the top of loaf.
4. Bake at 350°F 40 minutes, or until a cake tester inserted in center comes out clean. Serve warm.

Beer-Cheese Bread with Raisins

1 LOAF

1 cup raisins (5 ounces)
1 can or bottle (12 ounces)
beer
2½ cups all-purpose flour
¾ cup sugar
1 tablespoon baking powder
½ teaspoon baking soda
½ teaspoon salt
4 ounces Cheddar cheese,
finely shredded
¼ cup oil
1 egg

1. Heat raisins and beer to simmering. Remove from heat; let stand about 10 minutes.
2. Combine dry ingredients. Add cheese; stir to coat.
3. Mix oil and egg. Add to dry ingredients, along with beer and raisins. Beat just until blended.
4. Turn into a greased and floured 9x5x3-inch loaf pan.
5. Bake at 350°F 1 hour. Turn out on a rack to cool. Cool thoroughly before slicing.

Corn Bread I

ABOUT
16 PIECES

2 eggs
2 cups buttermilk
3 tablespoons shortening, melted
1½ teaspoons salt
2½ cups cornmeal
1 teaspoon baking powder
½ teaspoon baking soda

1. Beat eggs until light. Add buttermilk and melted shortening; mix well.
2. Mix dry ingredients together. Add to egg mixture; beat until smooth. Pour into a greased 9-inch square baking pan.
3. Bake at 375°F about 25 minutes. Serve hot.

Corn Bread II

ABOUT
8 SERVINGS

1 cup all-purpose flour
1 cup yellow cornmeal
2 teaspoons baking powder
½ teaspoon baking soda
1 teaspoon salt
1 cup milk
2½ teaspoons lime juice
1 egg, beaten
2 tablespoons lard, melted

1. Combine flour, cornmeal, baking powder, baking soda, and salt in a bowl.
2. Mix milk and lime juice; add to dry ingredients along with egg and lard. Mix well, but do not beat. Pour into a greased 11x7x1½-inch baking pan.
3. Bake at 450°F 15 to 20 minutes, or until it is brown and tests done. Cool slightly and cut into squares.

Corn Bread III

ABOUT
8 SERVINGS

1 cup all-purpose flour
1 cup yellow cornmeal
2 teaspoons baking powder
½ teaspoon baking soda
1 teaspoon salt
1 cup milk
2½ teaspoons lime juice
1 egg, beaten
2 tablespoons lard, melted

1. Combine flour, cornmeal, baking powder, baking soda, and salt in a bowl.
2. Mix milk and lime juice; add to dry ingredients along with egg and lard. Mix well, but do not beat. Pour into a greased 11x7x1½-inch baking pan.
3. Bake at 450°F 15 to 20 minutes, or until it is brown and tests done. Cool slightly and cut into squares.

Corn Bread III

Green
Chili
Cornbread

Green Chili Cornbread

8 TO 12
SERVINGS

4 ounces sharp Cheddar
  cheese (2 cups shredded)
2 green onions, trimmed and
  cut in 1-inch pieces
1 can (4 ounces) whole green
  chilies, drained and seeded
1 cup milk
1 egg
¼ cup vegetable oil
1¼ cups cornmeal
¾ cup flour
¼ cup sugar
1 tablespoon baking powder
½ teaspoon salt
1 can (8 ounces) whole
  kernel corn

1. Using **shredding disc** of food processor, shred cheese and set aside.
2. Using **steel blade,** process the green onions until finely chopped.
3. Add green chilies to green onions in bowl and process, in quick on/off motions, until finely chopped and set aside.
4. With **plastic blade** in bowl, add milk, egg, and oil, and process until blended. Add cornmeal, flour, sugar, baking powder, and salt and mix together for a few seconds. Add corn, green onions, and chilies.
5. Pour half of batter into a greased 9-inch square baking pan. Sprinkle with half of cheese. Repeat, using remaining batter and cheese.
6. Bake at 400°F about 35 to 40 minutes, or until lightly browned. Serve warm cut in squares.

Cheddar Cornbread

ABOUT
8 SERVINGS

1 cup yellow cornmeal
1 cup all-purpose flour
1 tablespoon baking powder
1 teaspoon salt
2 cups shredded Cheddar
  cheese (8 ounces)
1 cup milk
¼ cup melted butter or
  margarine or vegetable oil
1 egg
4 slices crisply cooked bacon,
  crumbled
1 green pepper, sliced
  (optional)

1. Combine cornmeal, flour, baking powder, salt, and 1 cup cheese in a mixing bowl.
2. Combine milk, butter, and egg in a separate bowl; beat well.
3. Add liquid ingredients to dry ingredients; stir just until flour is moistened. Pour into a greased 9-inch round layer cake pan. Sprinkle with remaining cheese and bacon. Top with green pepper rings, if desired.
4. Bake at 425°F 25 minutes, or until done.

Polish Christmas Bread

1 LOAF

5 eggs
2 cups confectioners' sugar
2¼ cups all-purpose flour
¾ cup finely chopped walnuts
⅔ cup raisins
4 ounces candied orange peel, finely chopped
2 teaspoons baking powder
½ teaspoon salt
1 cup butter or margarine (at room temperature)
1 tablespoon grated lemon peel
1 teaspoon vanilla extract
3 tablespoons vodka or brandy

1. Beat eggs with sugar 5 minutes at high speed of electric mixer.
2. Mix nuts, raisins, and orange peel with 2 tablespoons flour. Mix remaining flour with baking powder and salt.
3. Cream butter, lemon peel, and vanilla extract until fluffy. Beat in vodka. Add egg mixture gradually, beating constantly. Add flour mixture and beat 5 minutes. Fold fruit-nut mixture into the batter. Turn into a generously greased and floured 9x5x3-inch loaf pan or 1½-quart ring mold.
4. Bake at 350°F 1 hour.
5. Cool cake in pan on wire rack 10 minutes. Turn cake out onto rack; cool completely.
6. Wrap in plastic wrap. Store 1 or 2 days to mellow. Sprinkle with confectioners' sugar, if desired.

Pleasin' Pumpkin Bread

2 LOAVES

3½ cups all-purpose flour
3 cups sugar
2 cups cooked mashed pumpkin
1 cup vegetable oil
⅓ cup water
4 eggs
2 teaspoons baking soda
1½ teaspoons salt
2 teaspoons cinnamon
½ teaspoon nutmeg
¼ teaspoon cloves
¼ teaspoon ginger

1. Put flour, sugar, baking soda, salt, and spices into a large mixing bowl; mix well. Add pumpkin, oil, water, and eggs; beat until well blended.
2. Divide batter equally into 2 greased 9x5x3-inch loaf pans.
3. Bake at 350°F 70 minutes, or until done.
4. Cool before wrapping.

Irish Soda Bread with Currants

1 LARGE LOAF
SODA BREAD

4 cups sifted all-purpose flour
2 tablespoons sugar
2 teaspoons baking soda
1½ teaspoons salt
¼ cup butter or margarine
⅔ cup dried currants, plumped
½ cup white vinegar
1 cup milk

1. Mix flour, sugar, baking soda, and salt in a bowl. Cut in the butter with pastry blender or two knives until particles resemble rice kernels. Lightly mix in currants.
2. Mix vinegar and milk. Add half of the liquid to dry ingredients; blend quickly. Add remaining liquid and stir only until blended.
3. Turn dough onto floured surface. Lightly knead dough about 10 times and shape into a round loaf.
4. Bake at 375°F 35 to 40 minutes.

Irish Soda Bread

Rhubarb Bread

2 LOAVES

1½ cups firmly packed brown sugar
⅔ cup vegetable oil
1 cup buttermilk
1 egg
1 teaspoon vanilla extract
2½ cups all-purpose flour
1 teaspoon salt
1 teaspoon baking soda
1½ cups finely chopped rhubarb
½ cup chopped nuts
2 tablespoons sugar

1. Beat brown sugar, oil, buttermilk, egg, and vanilla extract in a mixing bowl.
2. Mix flour, salt, and baking soda. Add to brown sugar mixture and stir until blended.
3. Stir in rhubarb and nuts.
4. Turn into 2 greased 8x4x2-inch loaf pans. Sprinkle 1 tablespoon sugar over each.
5. Bake at 325°F 1 hour, or until done.

Zucchini Bread

1 LOAF

2 cups sugar
1 cup vegetable oil
3 eggs
1 teaspoon vanilla extract
3 cups all-purpose flour
1 teaspoon salt
1 teaspoon baking soda
1 teaspoon cinnamon
2 cups shredded unpeeled zucchini
1 cup chopped nuts

1. Beat sugar, oil, eggs, and vanilla extract in a mixing bowl until fluffy.
2. Mix flour, salt, baking soda, and cinnamon. Add to egg mixture and stir until blended.
3. Stir in zucchini and nuts.
4. Turn into a greased 9x5x3-inch loaf pan.
5. Bake at 350°F 1 hour and 20 minutes, or until done.
6. Cool before wrapping.

Buttermilk Coffeecake

1 COFFEECAKE

1 cup sugar
½ cup butter or margarine, softened
2 eggs
1 teaspoon vanilla extract
2 cups all-purpose flour
1 teaspoon baking powder
1 teaspoon baking soda
½ teaspoon salt
1 cup buttermilk

Topping:
1 cup chopped nuts
1 cup sugar
⅓ cup firmly packed brown sugar
1 teaspoon cinnamon
½ cup butter or margarine

1. Cream sugar and butter; beat in eggs and vanilla extract until well blended.
2. Combine flour, baking powder, baking soda, and salt.
3. Add buttermilk and flour mixture alternately to sugar mixture, beating well after each addition.
4. For topping, combine nuts, sugar, brown sugar, and cinnamon. Cut in butter.
5. Sprinkle half of topping mixture in bottom of a greased and floured 13x9x2-inch baking pan. Pour in batter. Cover with remaining topping.
6. Bake at 350°F 25 to 30 minutes.
7. Serve warm.

Whole Wheat Pear Bread

2 to 3 fresh Bartlett pears
2 tablespoons shortening
1 teaspoon grated lemon peel
⅔ cup firmly packed light
  brown sugar
½ cup honey
2 tablespoons lemon juice
⅓ cup water
1 egg, beaten
1 cup sifted enriched all-
  purpose flour
1 teaspoon baking soda
1 teaspoon salt
½ teaspoon ground
  cinnamon
¼ teaspoon ground cloves
1 cup whole wheat flour
1 cup chopped walnuts

1. Core pears, but do not peel. Cut lengthwise slices from one pear and reserve to decorate top. Dice enough remaining pears to measure 1 cup.
2. Mix shortening, grated lemon peel, and brown sugar in a bowl. Add honey, lemon juice, water, and egg; mix well.
3. Sift all-purpose flour, baking soda, salt, cinnamon, and cloves; stir in whole wheat flour. Add flour mixture to liquid mixture; stir just enough to moisten flour. Mix in walnuts and diced pears. Turn into a greased 9x5x3-inch loaf pan and arrange reserved pear slices crosswise along center.
4. Bake at 325°F 70 to 75 minutes.
5. Cool bread 10 minutes in pan on wire rack; remove from pan and cool completely before slicing or storing.

1 LOAF BREAD

Picnic Pear Nut Bread

Picnic Pear Nut Bread

1 LOAF

2 fresh fully ripe Bartlett
  pears
2 large eggs, beaten
1 cup whole bran
1½ cups sifted all-purpose
  flour
½ cup sugar
1 teaspoon baking powder
½ teaspoon salt
½ teaspoon baking soda
¼ cup soft shortening
½ cup chopped walnuts

1. Core and finely chop unpeeled pears to measure 1¼ cups. Combine with eggs and bran; let stand while preparing remaining ingredients.
2. Sift flour with sugar, baking powder, salt, and soda into mixing bowl. Add shortening and pear-bran mixture; mix until all of flour is moistened. Stir in walnuts. Turn into a well-greased 8½x4½x2½-inch loaf pan. Let stand 20 minutes.
3. Bake at 350°F about 1 hour, or until pick inserted in center comes out clean and dry. Let stand 10 minutes, then turn out onto wire rack to cool. If desired, spread with Lemon-Mint Butter.

Lemon-Mint Butter: Beat **1 cup softened butter or margarine** with **1 teaspoon grated lemon peel** and **2 tablespoons chopped fresh mint leaves.**

Grandma Louise's Banana Loaf

1 LOAF

1 cup sugar
½ cup shortening
1 cup mashed fully ripe
  bananas (2 to 3 bananas)
1 egg
¼ cup buttermilk
1¾ cups all-purpose flour
1½ teaspoons baking powder
1 teaspoon baking soda
½ teaspoon salt

1. Combine sugar, shortening, bananas, egg, and buttermilk in a mixing bowl; beat well.
2. Blend remaining ingredients, add to banana mixture, and mix until blended (about 1 minute).
3. Turn into a greaed 9x5x3-inch loaf pan.
4. Bake at 350°F 45 to 50 minutes, or until done.

Quick Buttermilk Bread

1 LOAF

1¾ cups all-purpose flour
2 teaspoons baking powder
¾ teaspoon baking soda
1 teaspoon salt
⅓ cup firmly packed brown
  sugar
1½ cups uncooked oats
1 cup buttermilk
½ cup vegetable oil
2 eggs, beaten
½ cup chopped pecans

1. Mix flour, baking powder, baking soda, and salt in a bowl. Stir in brown sugar and oats. Add remaining ingredients; stir only until dry ingredients are moistened.
2. Pour batter into a greased 9x5x3-inch loaf pan.
3. Bake at 350°F 50 to 55 minutes. Cool on wire rack about 10 minutes. Remove from pan; cool thoroughly.
4. Wrap and store. (Bread will slice better if stored a day before slicing.)

BISCUITS

Biscuits

ABOUT 1 DOZEN

2 cups all-purpose flour
1 tablespoon baking powder
1 teaspoon salt
⅓ cup butter or shortening
¾ cup milk

1. Combine flour, baking powder, and salt in a mixing bowl. Cut in butter with pastry blender or 2 knives until mixture resembles rice kernels.
2. Stir in milk with a fork just until mixture clings to itself.
3. Form dough into a ball and knead gently 8 to 10 times on lightly floured board. Gently roll dough ½ inch thick.
4. Cut with floured biscuit cutter or knife, using an even pressure to keep sides of biscuits straight.
5. Place on ungreased baking sheet, close together for soft-sided biscuits or 1 inch apart for crusty ones.
6. Bake at 450°F 10 to 15 minutes, or until golden brown.

Southern Buttermilk Biscuits: Follow recipe for Biscuits, substituting **buttermilk** for the milk and adding ¼ **teaspoon baking soda** to the dry ingredients and reducing baking powder to 2 teaspoons.

Drop Biscuits: Follow recipe for Biscuits, increasing milk to 1 cup. Omit rolling-out instructions. Simply drop from a spoon onto a lightly greased baking sheet.

Savory Biscuit Bread

6 SERVINGS

1½ cups all-purpose flour
1 tablespoon baking powder
½ teaspoon salt
½ teaspoon paprika
½ teaspoon celery salt
¼ teaspoon pepper
¼ teaspoon poultry seasoning
¼ cup shortening
½ cup milk (about)

1. Combine flour, baking powder, and seasonings in a mixing bowl. Cut in shortening until mixture resembles rice kernels.
2. Stir in milk with a fork just until flour is moistened.
3. Pat into a greased 8-inch round layer cake pan.
4. Bake at 450°F 10 to 15 minutes, or until done.

Biscuits Port-au-Prince

ABOUT
2 DOZEN
BISCUITS

2 cups sifted all-purpose
flour
2 teaspoons baking powder
1 teaspoon salt
5 tablespoons vegetable
shortening
¾ cup milk

1. Combine flour, baking powder, and salt in a bowl. Cut in shortening with pastry blender or two knives until mixture resembles small peas.
2. Make a well in center of mixture and add milk. Stir with fork until dough holds together.
3. Knead on a lightly floured board 30 seconds. Roll dough to ½-inch thickness. Cut with a floured 1½-inch cutter.
4. Place on greased baking sheets about 1 inch apart.
5. Bake at 425°F 15 to 20 minutes, or until golden brown.

Oatmeal Biscuits

ABOUT
16 BISCUITS

2 cups Basic Oats Mix (below)
½ cup cold milk

1. Combine Oats Mix and milk in a bowl; stir with a fork to a soft dough.
2. Turn dough onto a lightly floured surface. Knead with fingertips 10 times. Roll out to ½-inch thickness. Cut with a floured 2-inch round cutter. Put onto an ungreased cookie sheet.
3. Bake at 450°F 8 to 10 minutes.

Basic Oats Mix

9¾ CUPS MIX

6 cups sifted all-purpose
flour
¼ cup (4 tablespoons) baking powder
4 teaspoons salt
1⅓ cups shortening
2 cups quick or old-
fashioned oats, uncooked

1. Sift flour, baking powder, and salt together into large bowl. Cut in shortening until mixture resembles coarse crumbs. Stir in oats.
2. Store mixture in an airtight container in a cool, dry place until ready to use.

Scones

1 DOZEN

1⅔ cups all-purpose flour
1 tablespoon sugar
1½ teaspoons baking powder
½ teaspoon baking soda
½ teaspoon salt
½ cup shortening
½ cup buttermilk

1. Combine flour, sugar, baking powder, baking soda, and salt in a mixing bowl. Cut in shortening with pastry blender or two knives until mixture resembles rice kernels.
2. Stir in buttermilk with a fork until mixture clings to itself.
3. Form dough into a ball and knead gently about 8 times on a floured surface. Divide dough in half; roll each into a round about ½ inch thick. Cut each round into 6 wedge-shaped pieces. Place on ungreased baking sheets.
4. Bake at 450°F 8 to 10 minutes. Serve warm.

Biscuits and Muffins

MUFFINS

New England Blueberry Muffins

12 LARGE
MUFFINS

1 cup sugar
½ cup softened butter or
  margarine
2 eggs
½ cup milk
2 cups all-purpose flour
2 teaspoons baking powder
½ teaspoon salt
1 to 1½ cups fresh or frozen
  blueberries

1. Combine sugar, butter, eggs, and milk in a mixing bowl; beat well.
2. Blend flour, baking powder, and salt; add and mix until blended (about 1 minute). Fold in blueberries.
3. Spoon into 12 well-greased muffin cups, filling almost to the top of the cup.
4. Bake at 375°F 20 to 25 minutes.

Sunshine Corn Muffins

2 DOZEN

1½ cups all-purpose flour
1½ cups yellow cornmeal
1 tablespoon baking powder
⅛ teaspoon salt
1 cup milk
½ cup honey
½ cup vegetable oil
2 eggs

1. Combine dry ingredients in a mixing bowl.
2. Combine remaining ingredients in a separate bowl; beat well.
3. Add liquid ingredients to dry ingredients; stir just until flour is moistened. Spoon into 24 greased muffin-pan wells.
4. Bake at 400° 15 to 20 minutes, or until wooden pick inserted in muffin comes out clean.

Sunshine Cornbread: Follow recipe for Sunshine Corn Muffins, except pour mixture into a greased 9-inch square pan. Bake at 400°F 30 minutes, or until done.
6 SERVINGS

Lemon Chiffon Muffins

1 DOZEN

½ cup softened butter or
  margarine
½ cup sugar
Grated peel of 1 lemon
  (about 1 tablespoon)
2 tablespoons milk
2 eggs, separated
3 tablespoons lemon juice
  (about 1 lemon)
1 cup all-purpose flour
1 teaspoon baking powder
¼ teaspoon salt
¼ cup chopped nuts
1 tablespoon sugar
1 teaspoon nutmeg

1. Cream butter, sugar, lemon peel, milk, and egg yolks in a mixing bowl until light and fluffy. Beat in lemon juice.
2. Combine flour, baking powder, and salt in a separate bowl. Add to batter and mix just until blended.
3. Beat egg whites until soft peaks form; fold into batter.
4. Spoon into 12 greased muffin-pan wells. Sprinkle with a mixture of nuts, sugar, and nutmeg.
5. Bake at 375°F 15 to 20 minutes, or until done.

Hot Cross Fruit Muffins

1 DOZEN

2 cups biscuit mix
3 tablespoons sugar
½ to ¾ teaspoon ground cardamom
½ cup dark or golden raisins
¼ cup chopped citron
1 egg, well beaten
⅔ cup milk
2 tablespoons melted shortening, or cooking or salad oil
Frosting, below

1. Mix the biscuit mix, sugar, and cardamom in a bowl; sir in the raisins and citron.
2. Blend the egg, milk, and shortening thoroughly. Add to dry ingredients; stir quickly and lightly until dry ingredients and barely moistened. Spoon batter into greased 2½-inch muffin-pan wells.
3. Bake at 400°F about 15 minutes.
4. Meanwhile, prepare Frosting.
5. Remove muffins from pan to wire rack; cool slightly. Then form a cross on each muffin, using the frosting.

Frosting: Beat together until smooth ½ **cup plus 2 tablespoons confectioners' sugar, 2 teaspoons water, ¼ teaspoon vanilla extract,** and **1 tablespoon almond paste.**

Maple Tree Muffins

1 DOZEN

2 cups all-purpose flour
1 tablespoon baking powder
½ teaspoon salt
½ cup chopped nuts
⅔ cup milk
½ cup pure maple syrup or maple-blended syrup
1 egg
¼ cup vegetable oil

1. Combine flour, baking powder, salt, and nuts in a mixing bowl.
2. Combine remaining ingredients in a separate bowl; beat well.
3. Add liquid ingredients to dry ingredients; stir just until flour is moistened. Spoon into 12 greased muffin-pan wells.
4. Bake at 400°F 15 to 20 minutes, or until a wooden pick inserted in muffin comes out clean.

Dakota Bran Muffins

1 DOZEN

1 cup all-purpose flour
1 tablespoon baking powder
½ teaspoon salt
1½ cups ready-to-eat bran flakes
1 cup milk
1 egg
¼ cup vegetable oil
¼ cup honey or sugar

1. Combine dry ingredients in a mixing bowl.
2. Combine remaining ingredients in a separate bowl; beat well.
3. Add liquid ingredients to dry ingredients; stir just until flour is moistened. Spoon batter into 12 greased muffin-pan wells.
4. Bake at 400°F 20 to 25 minutes, or until golden brown.

Bran-Oatmeal Muffins

1 DOZEN

¾ cup bran cereal
¾ cup milk
¼ cup butter or margarine
¼ cup molasses
1 egg
1 cup all-purpose flour
2 tablespoons sugar
1 teaspoon baking powder
½ teaspoon baking soda
½ teaspoon salt
1 cup uncooked oats

1. Combine bran cereal and milk to soften.
2. Beat butter and molasses together in a bowl. Add egg and mix well. Add bran-milk mixture.
3. Mix flour, sugar, baking powder, baking soda, and salt. Add dry ingredients to bran mixture; stir just until moistened, Stir in oats.
4. Spoon mixture into 12 greased medium-sized muffin-pan wells.
5. Bake at 400°F 15 to 18 minutes, or until golden-brown.

Oatmeal Muffins

**2 cups plus 2 tablespoons
  Basic Oats Mix (page 67)
¼ cup sugar
1 cup milk
1 egg, beaten**

1. Combine Oats Mix and sugar in a bowl. Add milk and egg; stir until just blended.
2. Fill 12 greased 2½-inch muffin-pan wells ⅔ full.
3. Bake at 400°F about 20 minutes, or until golden brown.
12 MUFFINS

Basic Oats Mix, Oatmeal Biscuits, Oatmeal Muffins

PANCAKES, WAFFLES, and POPOVERS

Pancakes

ABOUT
12 PANCAKES

1½ cups sifted all-purpose
    flour
1 tablespoon sugar
1½ teaspoons baking powder
¼ teaspoon salt
2 egg yolks, beaten
1⅓ cups milk
2 tablespoons butter or
    margarine, melted
2 egg whites

1. Start heating griddle or heavy skillet over low heat.
2. Mix flour, sugar, baking powder, and salt in a bowl.
3. Combine egg yolks, milk, and butter. Add liquid to flour mixture and beat until blended.
4. Beat egg whites until rounded peaks are formed. Spread beaten egg whites over batter and fold gently together.
5. Test griddle; it is hot enough for baking when drops of water sprinkled on surface dance in small beads. Lightly grease griddle, if so directed by manufacturer.
6. Pour batter onto griddle into pools about 4 inches in diameter, leaving at least 1 inch between cakes. Turn pancakes as they become puffy and full of bubbles. Turn only once.
7. Serve hot.

Buttermilk Pancakes: Follow recipe for Pancakes; substitute ½ **teaspoon baking soda** for the baking powder and **buttermilk** for the milk. Do not separate eggs. Beat eggs with buttermilk and proceed as in step 3 above.

Cornmeal Pancakes: Follow recipe for Pancakes. Decrease flour to ¾ cup. Mix ¾ **cup yellow cornmeal** into dry ingredients.

Rye Pancakes: Follow recipe for Buttermilk Pancakes. Decrease flour to ¾ cup and mix in ¾ **cup rye flour.** Blend **3 tablespoons molasses** into buttermilk-egg mixture.

Blueberry Pancakes: Follow recipe for Pancakes; gently fold **2 cups rinsed and drained blueberries** into batter after folding in beaten egg whites.

Petite Pancake Puffs

3 DOZEN
PANCAKES

1½ cups all-purpose flour
2 tablespoons sugar
1 teaspoon baking powder
1 teaspoon baking soda
1 teaspoon salt
1¾ cups buttermilk
3 egg yolks
1 teaspoon vanilla extract
3 tablespoons butter or
    margarine, melted and
    cooled completely
1 cup dark seedless or
    golden raisins, plumped
3 egg whites

1. Blend the flour, sugar, baking powder, baking soda, and salt in a large bowl; set aside.
2. Beat the buttermilk, egg yolks, extract, and butter until well mixed. Add to dry ingredients all at one time; beat thoroughly. Stir in the raisins.
3. Beat the egg whites until stiff, not dry, peaks are formed. Fold into the batter.
4. For each pancake, spoon 1 tablespoon batter onto a heated griddle or skillet and spread into a 3-inch round. Turn each pancake as it becomes full of bubbles; continue baking until lightly browned.
5. Transfer pancakes to a heated platter and immediately brush with **melted butter;** keep warm. Sprinkle pancakes with **confectioners' sugar.** Serve with heated **maple-blended syrup.**

Waffles

ABOUT
4 LARGE
WAFFLES

2 cups sifted all-purpose
  flour
1 tablespoon sugar
1 tablespoon baking powder
½ teaspoon salt
3 eggs, well-beaten
2 cups milk
½ cup butter or margarine,
  melted

1. Mix flour, sugar, baking powder, and salt in a bowl.
2. Combine eggs, milk, and melted butter. Add liquid mixture to flour mixture; beat just until batter is blended.
3. Heat waffle baker. Pour enough batter into waffle baker to allow spreading to within 1 inch of edges. Lower cover and bake waffle; do not raise cover during baking. Lift cover and loosen waffle with a fork. Serve hot.

Buttermilk Waffles: Follow recipe for Waffles; substitute **buttermilk** for milk. Decrease baking powder to 2 teaspoons and add **1 teaspoon baking soda.**

Wheat Germ Pecan Waffles: Follow recipe for Waffles; decrease flour to 1½ cups. Stir ½ **cup toasted wheat germ** into the flour mixture. Sprinkle **3 tablespoons coarsely chopped pecans** onto the batter before baking each waffle.

Cheese Waffles: Follow recipe for Waffles. When batter is smooth, blend in ½ **cup shredded cheese.**

Chocolate Waffles: Follow recipe for Waffles. Generously sprinkle **semisweet chocolate pieces** over batter before closing waffle baker.

Popovers

8 POPOVERS

3 eggs
1 cup milk
2 tablespoons vegetable oil
½ teaspoon salt
1 cup sifted all-purpose flour

1. Beat eggs in a mixing bowl. Beat in milk, oil, and salt.
2. Beat in flour until mixture is smooth and well blended.
3. For best results, preheat iron popover pan after thoroughly coating pan wells with shortening or oil. Pour batter into 8 popover-pan wells or 8 greased heat-resistant custard cups.
4. Bake at 400°F 35 to 40 minutes, or until popovers are puffed and golden brown. Serve hot with butter.

Note: For a crispier popover, make slit in side of each baked popover to allow the steam to escape. Return popovers to oven for 10 minutes with the heat turned off.

Whole Wheat Popovers

6 POPOVERS

⅔ cup all-purpose flour
⅓ cup whole wheat flour
¼ teaspoon salt
2 eggs (about ½ cup)
1 cup milk
1 tablespoon melted
  shortening

1. Mix the flours and salt in a bowl. Add a mixture of eggs, milk, and melted shortening; beat until thoroughly blended.
2. Pour batter into ungreased 5-ounce heat-resistant glass custard cups until each is half full.
3. Bake at 450°F 15 minutes; reduce oven temperature to 350°F and bake 35 minutes. Serve hot.

JIFFY QUICK BREADS

Poppy Seed Cheese Bread

ABOUT
6 SERVINGS

1 cup shredded Cheddar
cheese (about 4 ounces)
1 cup all-purpose biscuit mix
⅓ cup milk
1 egg
¼ cup chopped onion
1 tablespoon poppy seed

1. Combine ½ cup cheese and biscuit mix in a mixing bowl.
2. Add milk; stir just until flour is moistened. Pat dough over bottom of a greased 8- or 9-inch pie plate.
3. Combine remaining cheese, egg, and onion. Spread over biscuit dough. Sprinkle with poppy seed.
4. Bake at 425°F 15 to 20 minutes.

Garlic Bread

ABOUT
1 DOZEN
SLICES

1 loaf French bread
½ cup butter or margarine,
softened
¼ teaspoon garlic powder or
garlic salt

1. Slice bread almost through to bottom crust at 1-inch intervals.
2. Thoroughly combine butter and garlic powder. Spread on both sides of each bread slice.
3. Place on baking sheet.
4. Bake at 350°F 15 to 20 minutes, or until hot and crispy.

Sesame Seed Twists

2 DOZEN
TWISTS

2 cups biscuit mix
¼ cup chilled butter
3 tablespoons melted butter
2 tablespoons sesame seed
1 egg yolk
1 teaspoon milk

1. Prepare biscuit mix as directed on package for rolled biscuits. Roll out on a lightly floured surface into a 12-inch square.
2. Thinly slice 3 tablespoons of butter and place on half of dough; fold other half over it. With rolling pin, gently seal open edges. Repeat procedure, using remaining chilled butter. Fold other half over, forming a 6-inch square.
3. Roll dough into a 12-inch square. Divide in half. Set one half in refrigerator.
4. Brush surface with melted butter. Sprinkle with some of the sesame seed. Cut into twelve 6x1-inch strips. Twist each strip and place on an ungreased baking sheet. Brush with mixture of egg yolk and milk. Sprinkle with more sesame seed. Repeat with other half.
5. Bake at 425°F 10 minutes.

La Verde Slices

ABOUT
1 DOZEN
SLICES

1 loaf Italian bread, cut
diagonally in 1-inch slices
½ cup softened butter or
margarine
2 tablespoons finely chopped
green pepper
2 tablespoons finely chopped
onion

1. Broil bread slices until golden brown on each side.
2. Combine butter, green pepper, and onion. Spread on one side of each slice.
3. Broil until lightly browned.

Jiffy Beer Bread

3 cups self-rising flour
3 tablespoons sugar
1 can or bottle (12 ounces)
  beer

1. Mix self-rising flour and sugar; make a well in center.
2. Add beer. Stir until just blended.
3. Turn into a greased 9x5x3-inch loaf pan.
4. Bake at 350°F 50 minutes, or until done. Turn out immediately. Cool on a rack.

Quick Strips

ABOUT
20 STRIPS

1 loaf unsliced white bread
½ cup butter or margarine,
  melted
¼ teaspoon garlic salt
Grated Parmesan cheese,
  sesame seed, or poppy seed

1. Cut flour 1¼-inch slices from loaf of bread. Cut each slice into 1-inch strips.
2. Combine butter and garlic salt in a 13x9x2-inch baking pan.
3. Toss bread strips in butter; sprinkle with cheese.
4. Bake at 350°F 20 minutes.

Homemade Croutons

Day-old bread slices
Softened butter or margarine

1. Spread both sides of bread slices with butter.
2. Stack slices and cut into cubes.
3. Spread over baking sheet.
4. Bake at 275°F 25 to 35 minutes, stirring occasionally, until dry and lightly browned.

Parmesan Croutons: Follow recipe for Homemade Croutons, except sprinkle both sides of bread with **grated Parmesan cheese** before cubing and baking.

Crusty Croutons: Follow recipe for Homemade Croutons except use **French bread** slices instead of day-old bread slices and do not cube bread. Turn slices over once during baking.

Croutons for Fruit Soups

ABOUT
14 TO 18

4 stale dinner rolls or slices
   baba or bread
½ cup whipping cream
2 tablespoons butter or
   margarine
¼ cup confectioners' sugar

1. Cut rolls into 1-inch cubes.
2. Dip cubes in cream; quickly sauté in butter.
3. Dust with confectioners' sugar.

Sugar Buns

1 DOZEN BUNS

1 cup firmly packed brown
   sugar
⅓ cup butter or margarine
1 tablespoon corn syrup
½ cup chopped pecans
2 cans refrigerated dough
   for butterflake dinner rolls

1. Combine brown sugar, butter, and corn syrup in a saucepan; bring to boiling, stirring occasionally.
2. Stir in pecans.
3. Divide mixture evenly among 12 muffin-pan wells.
4. Place 2 rolls in each cup.
5. Bake at 375°F 15 minutes. Remove from pans immediately.

Cranberry Swirl Rolls

ABOUT
2 DOZEN ROLLS

1 package (about 14 ounces)
   hot roll mix
1 can (16 ounces) jellied
   cranberry sauce
¼ cup firmly packed brown
   sugar
1 teaspoon cinnamon

1. Prepare hot roll mix following package directions.
2. Roll half of dough at a time into a 12x8-inch rectangle. Spread each rectangle with cranberry sauce to within 1 inch of edge. Sprinkle with brown sugar and cinnamon. Starting with a 12-inch side, roll up jelly-roll fashion. Seal edges. Cut each into 1-inch slices and place cut-side down on greased baking sheets.
3. Bake at 375°F 10 minutes, or until done.

Streusel Coffeecake

1 COFFEECAKE

Coffeecake:
2 cups all-purpose biscuit
   mix
½ cup sugar
⅔ cup beer
1 egg, slightly beaten

Topping:
½ cup flour
⅓ cup sugar
1 teaspoon cinnamon
⅓ cup butter or margarine

1. For coffeecake, combine biscuit mix and sugar. Mix beer and egg.
2. Add beer mixture to dry mixture. Stir lightly, just until moistened. Turn into a greased 9-inch round cake pan.
3. For streusel topping, combine flour, sugar, and cinnamon. Cut in butter until crumbly. Sprinkle over coffeecake batter.
4. Bake at 400°F 25 minutes. Serve warm or cooled.

Cinnamon Swirl Date Ring

ONE
COFFEE RING

3 cups all-purpose biscuit
  mix
¼ cup sugar
¼ cup butter or margarine
¾ cup milk
Cinnamon-Date Filling

1. Combine biscuit mix and sugar in a mixing bowl; cut in butter until mixture resembles rice kernels.
2. Gently stir in milk just until ingredients are moistened.
3. Drop half of dough by tablespoonfuls into a greased 6-cup ring mold. Sprinkle with Cinnamon-Date Filling. Top with remaining dough.
4. Bake at 350°F 25 to 30 minutes, or until a wooden pick inserted in cake comes out clean. Invert mold onto plate; leave over cake 5 minutes. Serve warm.

DOUGHNUTS

Filled Berlin Doughnuts

ABOUT
2 DOZEN

1 package active dry yeast
¼ cup warm water
½ cup sugar
1 teaspoon salt
⅓ cup butter
1 tablespoon orange juice
2 teaspoons rum extract
1 cup milk, scalded
3½ to 4 cups all-purpose
  flour
2 eggs, well beaten
Fat for deep frying heated to
  375°F
Jam or jelly

1. Soften yeast in the warm water.
2. Put ½ cup sugar, the salt, butter, orange juice and rum extract into a large bowl. Pour scalded milk over ingredients in bowl. Stir until butter is melted. Cool to lukewarm.
3. Blend in 1 cup of the flour and beat until smooth. Stir in yeast. Add about half of the remaining flour and beat until smooth. Beat in the eggs. Then beat in enough of the remaining flour to make a soft dough.
4. Turn dough onto a lightly floured surface and let rest 5 to 10 minutes.
5. Knead until smooth and elastic. Form into a ball and put into a greased deep bowl; turn dough to bring greased surface to top. Cover; let rise in a warm place until double in bulk.
6. Punch down dough. Turn dough onto a lightly floured surface and roll ½ inch thick. Cut dough into rounds with a 3-inch cutter. Cover with waxed paper and let rise on rolling surface away from drafts and direct heat, until double in bulk (30 to 45 minutes).
7. About 20 minutes before deep frying, heat fat.
8. Fry doughnuts in heated fat. Put in only as many doughnuts at one time as will float uncrowded one layer deep in the fat. Fry 2 to 3 minutes, or until lightly browned; turn doughnuts with a fork or tongs when they rise to the surface and several times during cooking (do not pierce). Lift from fat; drain over fat for a few seconds before removing to absorbent paper. Cool.
9. Cut a slit through to the center in the side of each doughnut. Force about ½ teaspoon jam or jelly into center and press lightly to close slit. (A pastry bag and tube may be used to force jelly or jam into slit.) Shake 2 or 3 Bismarcks at one time in bag containing **sugar**.

Drop Doughnuts

ABOUT
30 DOUGHNUTS

4 eggs
1 cup buttermilk
2 teaspoons vanilla extract
1 teaspoon grated lemon or
   orange peel (optional)
3 cups all-purpose flour
1½ teaspoons baking powder
Cooking oil for deep frying
Honey
Cinnamon

1. Beat eggs; stir in buttermilk, vanilla extract, and grated peel. Combine flour and baking powder. Stir into the egg mixture. Cover with a cloth. Let stand at room temperature for 1 hour.
2. In a deep fryer, heat oil to 375°F. Drop batter by the tablespoon. Cook 4 minutes, or until doughnuts are golden brown. Drain on paper towels. Drizzle with honey and sprinkle with cinnamon. Serve hot.

Note: Batter keeps well in the refrigerator. Bring to room temperature before cooking.

Lemon Doughnut Balls

ABOUT
3 DOZEN

2 cups all-purpose flour
¼ cup sugar
1 tablespoon baking powder
1 teaspoon salt
½ teaspoon baking soda
½ cup milk
¼ cup melted butter or
   margarine
2 tablespoons grated lemon
   peel
¼ cup lemon juice
1 egg
½ cup flaked coconut
Vegetable oil or shortening
   heated to 375°F
Confectioner's sugar

1. Combine flour, sugar, baking powder, salt, and baking soda in a mixing bowl.
2. Combine milk, butter, lemon peel and juice, egg, and coconut in a separate bowl; beat well.
3. Add liquid ingredients to dry ingredients. Stir just until flour is moistened.
4. Drop by teaspoonfuls into hot oil. Fry 3 minutes, or until golden brown. Drain on paper towels. Sprinkle with confectioners' sugar.

Index